N/H

HOW TO BRING UP PLANTS

Alec Bristow

HOW TO
BRING UP PLANTS

HARVILL PRESS
8 Grafton Street, London W1
1983

Harvill Press and William Collins Sons & Company Limited
London · Glasgow · Sydney · Auckland
Toronto · Johannesburg

British Library Cataloguing in Publication Data

Bristow, Alec
How to bring up plants.
1. Plants, cultivated
I. Title
635   SB91

ISBN 0-00-262304-8

First published 1983
© Alec Bristow 1983
Illustrations by Merrily Harpur
Diagrams by Carol Johnson

Photoset in Linotron Sabon by
Rowland Phototypesetting Ltd
Bury St Edmunds, Suffolk
Made and printed in Great Britain by
William Collins Sons & Co. Ltd, Glasgow

To Carol O'Brien
who helped to bring this book to birth

CONTENTS

INTRODUCTION

DURING RECENT TIMES there have been just as many discoveries about the best way to bring up plants as there have about the best way to bring up babies. Yet the results of this knowledge are much more apparent among our children than among our plants.

The gardens of the past, like the nurseries of the past, were rigid authoritarian affairs. They were presided over by head gardeners who were in their attitude – and to judge from old pictures even in their facial expression – just like those dragons of governesses who spent their time instilling fear both into their tender young charges and into their own underlings who did the actual dirty work.

Discipline was the order of the day. Indoors and out, young growing things were expected to conform uncomplainingly to strict rules and regulations. Disobedience was the gravest of sins, and unruly behaviour was swiftly followed by severe treatment, which usually took the form – figuratively with children and literally with plants – of being cut down to size.

In the nineteenth century the rich landowners competed with each other to display their wealth not only in the size and grandeur of their houses and estates but in the number of servants they employed – and the best way to demonstrate this in the garden was to make it as formal and artificial as possible, so that it was obvious to any visitor that a whole army of gardeners must be needed to keep the place in order. The miles of trim hedges, the billiard-table lawns, the yews and box trees clipped into cones and globes and animals and birds, were the outdoor equivalent of the trim nurseries and tidy schoolrooms.

There was during that period stern moral disapproval of two things: idleness and nature. Countless grim sermons and improving tracts were based upon the text 'Satan finds mischief for idle hands to do'. As for nature, was it not rooted in Original Sin, and therefore never to be given in to but always to be overcome? The matter was put clearly and firmly in Mrs Beeton's *Book of*

Household Management, first published in 1861. A section devoted to the duties of nursemaids begins with the words: 'Most
children have some bad habit, of which they must be broken.'
What went for nurseries went for gardens too. Nature had to be
tamed.

As more and more has been found out about the true nature and
needs of children, this rigid attitude has been relaxed. This is
partly because a softer approach makes for a pleasanter life for all
concerned, but also because it has been realized that giving
growing things the care they need enables them to grow better and
realize their full potential. Some people would say that this softer
approach has gone too far, that permissiveness has destroyed all
sense of value. Few, however, would want to go back to the
stifling regimentation of the past.

At the same time gardeners are beginning to adopt a more
live-and-let-live approach towards their plants. Recent discoveries by botanists and plant scientists working in research stations
have given us new insights into the way plants grow. Many
gardeners are still obsessed with rules and regulations, however,
largely because of ignorance. Within the home they are aware of
recent advances in infant care, but once in the garden they return
to the rigid attitudes of the past, based upon trying to overcome
nature rather than understand it. They work long and hard at
harsh, disciplinary tasks – lopping, pruning, trimming, restricting – in the frame of mind of the Victorian father who, when
beating his children, would say, 'This hurts me more than it hurts
you.'

The modern tendency in child care is to enjoy your children, to
be a companion to them rather than a tyrant. It is to help you to
bring the same understanding to your plants, and so get the same
companionship and enjoyment from them, that this book is
written.

CHAPTER ONE
How plants begin life

TO PREPARE FOR the task of looking after young plants, it is helpful to understand something of the processes that bring them into being.

SEXUAL REPRODUCTION

Where flowering plants are concerned – and that includes the vast majority of those which we grow in our garden and homes – the answer is sex. Sexual reproduction is what divides the higher from the lower forms of life. It is the most primitive forms of life that are sexless (though, as we shall see, there are some plants so degenerate that they have actually given up sex).

The bright colours and delicious scents of our favourite flowers are all designed for one purpose: to achieve sexual fulfilment for the plant by attracting a host of different creatures – bees, butterflies, moths, humming birds and many others – to carry pollen from the male to the female organs and so bring about fertilization. If all goes well this is followed, after the necessary period of gestation, by the production of seed, from which a new generation will arise.

The result of all this sexual activity is to create almost endless variety – in fact variety is what sex is all about. Just as no two children in a human family are exactly alike, so each seedling, even from a crossing of the same parents, is an individual with its own personal characteristics. Some are bright, others drab; some easy, others difficult; some bouncing with health, others sickly; some refined, others coarse. True, with certain plants modern breeders have been able, by continuous inbreeding for generation after generation, to produce what they call 'pure lines' – that is to say assemblages of standard offspring apparently identical in every respect. But even among these the odd individual will appear from time to time that is markedly different from the rest.

That is why seed raisers employ people to keep constant watch for nonconformist plants, and to root them out and destroy them before they can contaminate the rest. This rooting is called 'roguing', and the plant that differs from its fellows is called a 'rogue'.

Such ruthlessly imposed uniformity amounts to the deliberate frustration of the sexual method of propagation. The whole natural process of development of the ancestors of our cultivated plants, as of our own ancestors, has relied on the rich variety continually created by sexual coupling. The better adapted of these varied offspring have survived, while the less well adapted have disappeared. Once variety is lost, there is really not much point in sex any more.

However, conditions in the wild are very different from those in gardens – let alone in greenhouses and homes. In the wild, conditions can change drastically, sometimes over quite short periods of time. The environment may suddenly become hotter or colder, wetter or drier. After such changes the large conservative majority of plants of an established species, hardly distinguishable from each other and safely settled in their ways, may find life very uncomfortable. Then the future of the species may well depend on a chance unorthodox seedling that by virtue of some unusual characteristic can adapt itself to the new conditions which its normal fellows cannot survive.

With cultivated plants things are different. In the garden the rigours of nature can be softened to a large extent: the effects of droughts can be mitigated by watering, the effects of floods by draining; protection can be given against damage by cold or heat; diseases and pests can be controlled by chemical and other means; competition from weeds can be eliminated, or at least reduced, by hand-pulling, hoeing or the use of herbicides. Indoors, whether in the greenhouse or in the home, complete protection can be given against nearly all the forces of nature that threaten a plant's well-being.

In such circumstances variety, the spice of sexual reproduction, is no longer needed in the same way. That is one reason why seedsmen's lists offer far fewer varieties for sale than they used to do. Another reason, of course, is that it is more profitable to concentrate on a limited number of standard bestsellers than to carry a wide range containing many less popular kinds.

Plant spotting – or the use of élites

In the old days the creation of a new variety was very much a matter of chance: the bees and the pollen were left to get on with it, and the occasional lucky accident happened in the form of a seedling that was different, and sometimes better as well. Plant-breeders at first were simply plant-spotters: they kept their eyes open for superior specimens of plants, and chose these superior specimens for cultivation in gardens. To start with, when plants were cultivated to eat, not to look at, they would choose those which gave the highest yield. Later, when gardens began to provide satisfaction for the eye as well as the stomach, specimens of greater aesthetic appeal were chosen too.

Superior individuals selected for growing in this way are known to plant-breeders as élites. When the breeding of plants began to be studied and practised, élitism had not become the term of abuse that it is today. In the world of plants superiority was simply accepted as the basis for good breeding.

The first step towards the improvement of a natural population of plants is to choose a number of élite individuals, take the seeds from them, mix them and sow them. If this process is continued, the whole population may over a period of time be changed in the desired direction. This process of mass selection is an effective way to start to improve and purify cross-fertilized plants, such as petunias and cabbages; it is also used to keep established strains on the path of purity.

However, even the most nearly pure populations sometimes produce a proportion of plants untrue to type. Continual careful selection may reduce the number, but there is always the risk that cross-fertilization by inferior types, either cultivated or wild, will spoil the purity from time to time. One way to prevent this is to self-fertilize the élite plants which provide the seed, so that none of their offspring can have an undesirable as its father. But this is not always easy, because on the whole plants prefer to cross with strangers. Besides, continual self-fertilization is likely to lead to loss of vigour.

Selecting the élites on the basis of appearance alone is danger-ous, because appearances can be very misleading. Every plant, like every person, has a dual personality: an outward and visible set of characteristics (known to geneticists as its *phenotype*) and another hidden set (its *genotype*) representing the secret genetic code carried in every one of its cells from the moment when the sperm fused with the egg at the time of fertilization. Sometimes the two personalities may be alike in a particular characteristic: just as a blue-eyed person is pure in respect of that colour and can only produce blue-eyed offspring when mated with another blue-eyed person, so a dwarf pea is pure in respect of height and can only produce dwarf offspring when crossed with another dwarf.

A brown-eyed person, on the other hand, may be pure in respect of that colour, in which case all the offspring will be brown-eyed, or impure, in which case the hidden character may assert itself in the form of blue-eyed progeny, even after mating with an impure brown-eyed partner; if the partner is pure, all the offspring will be brown-eyed. Similarly, a pure-bred tall pea can only produce tall progeny, but an impure one may give rise to a dwarf or two. The reason is that blue eyes in humans and dwarfness in peas are *recessive* (i.e. they only show themselves in individuals pure for that character), while brown eyes and tallness are dominant (i.e. they will show themselves even in impure individuals).

Though still an artist, the modern plant-breeder has had to become a scientist too. He studies the results of the latest genetic research; he pores over statistical tables; he peers through microscopes at sections of cells to examine and count the chromosomes which carry the genes that determine all the characteristics of plants, seen and unseen.

A great deal still remains to be discovered, of course, and in time new knowledge of genetics will no doubt be reflected in the creation of totally new varieties of plants for our gardens and our homes. A considerable amount has already been done, however, since the year 1900, when the rediscovery of a neglected paper published thirty-four years before by the Austrian friar and amateur botanist Gregor Mendel started the modern science of genetics by demonstrating the split personality of plants (later found to apply to animals, including ourselves). The idea of dual nature was in the air at the time: Freud was discovering the unconscious half of our make-up, and it was only a few years before that Robert Louis Stevenson had put the notion of split personality on the map with Dr Jekyll and Mr Hyde.

It was soon realized that what was most important about a plant from the breeding point of view was its genetic make-up. But how could it be investigated? The answer was to examine a plant's offspring to see whether they were like the parent, and if not how they differed and in what proportions. By means of large numbers of careful crosses, the results of which can be both statistically analysed according to the laws of genetics and studied by examining cells under the microscope, it has been possible to form a complete picture of the genetic make-up of all our important food crops and ornamental plants, as well as a great many of their wild ancestors and relations – the value of which to breeding we shall soon see.

In selecting single plants, the most useful way to identify superior genotypes is to choose a large number of élite individuals out of a mixed population, self-fertilize them and grow the offspring of each élite as a separate group. Doing this with recessive characters presents no problem: as the parent is pure, the offspring must be just like it. With dominant characters things are not so easy. Mixed progeny must be counted and the proportions showing different characteristics analysed statistically; from the figures experts can work out with great accuracy the genetic constitution of the plant.

What is the practical effect of all this knowledge and technique as far as the amateur plant-lover is concerned? The good news is that many greatly improved varieties have been, and are still being, produced. The sad news is that it has become almost impossible for even the most enthusiastic amateur plant-breeder to compete with the professionals in attempting to produce something better than, or even as good as, existing varieties.

Resistance to self-fertilization

One problem for all concerned is the very stubborn resistance shown by some plants towards any attempt at self-fertilization. Cabbages, for instance, cannot normally be induced to set seed from their own pollen, which is simply unable to push its way down into the ovary to bring about sexual union. No doubt the taboo against self-fertilization was useful during the course of evolution to ensure cross-breeding, and to break such a deep-seated taboo may be extremely difficult. Determined plant-breeders have, however, discovered certain ways to overcome resistance by artificial insemination, using such techniques as bud-pollination, in which impregnation is performed surgically, before the flower has opened and had time to develop its defences.

Further inbreeding may be brought about by what is called brother-sister mating, i.e. by crossing offspring from the same act of fertilization. In most cases resistance to this form of pairing is not so strong as that against self-fertilization. The immediate results of brother-sister mating may be to produce a large proportion of deformed or otherwise abnormal offspring. However, if the abnormal progeny are destroyed as soon as they appear there will be fewer of them in each succeeding generation, until the harmful recessive genes responsible for the abnormalities will eventually be bred out and a uniform strain established.

Many of our most useful and beautiful cultivated plants have been developed by such methods. They are the thoroughbreds, a triumph of human technology. But thoroughbreds have their own very considerable problems. The extreme refinement so painstakingly achieved may have left them with a delicate constitution, so that they cannot put up with the conditions in which their more robust ancestors thrived. Their resistance may be low. They may suffer from what is known as 'inbreeding depression'.

Back-crossing to overcome weaknesses

To overcome such problems it may be necessary to bring in a drop or two of common blood. One way to do this is by 'back-crossing', in which a highly bred plant, which may have achieved perfection in all respects but one (say disease resistance, strength of stem, or earliness of flowering), is mated with a natural, unrefined specimen of the parent species which possesses the missing character. Sometimes such back-crossing has to be carried out over many generations before the desired parental attribute is transferred to the progeny without taking away their thoroughbred qualities.

To combat susceptibility to attacks by disease or pests among some cultivated plants, increasing use is being made of mating not with the parent species but with others less closely related. Some new breeds of potato have built-in resistance to attacks by blight and eelworm by virtue of the inclusion in their parentage of wild species of *Solanum*; these do not have even remotely edible tubers but do have excellent natural defences against those two plagues.

F_1 hybrids

Another technique developed over recent years has managed to combine this mongrel toughness – 'hybrid vigour' as it is called – with pure breeding. What happens is that two pure lines are established by a process of inbreeding and grown in isolation from each other. When mating time comes, the two lines are crossed (in many cases by hand, the pollen being transferred to the receptive stigma by means of a soft brush). The seed resulting from this arranged marriage is sold – at a considerably higher price than ordinary seed – in packets labelled 'F_1 hybrid', the designation F_1 standing for Filial 1, meaning simply 'first generation'.

These 'thoroughbred mongrels' are not only very much more vigorous than their inbred parents but extremely uniform in appearance and qualities. Many crops of great economic importance, such as tomatoes, sweet corn and onions, have been transformed by the introduction of F_1 hybrids, which are capable of giving yields three or four times greater than even the best varieties produced by old-fashioned methods. Certain totally new things have been created which would not have been possible, or even conceivable, in the days before the development of F_1 breeding techniques: for instance the modern all-female cucumbers, which produce only sweet, seedless fruits because there are no male flowers to make a nuisance of themselves by fertilizing them and turning them hard and bitter.

So successful have F_1 hybrids been that many commercial growers of food crops now grow nothing else. And more and more F_1 varieties are now appearing in seedsmen's lists for sale to the ordinary amateur gardener, who is beginning to find that the extra cost is more than made up for by the superior results. It is possible that within a few years only F_1 hybrids of certain vegetables will be available, because there will be little or no call for the old-fashioned varieties. That will not necessarily mean having to go on paying a stiff price to make up for all the hand work involved in pollination: in many cases that can now be left to the unpaid work of bees and other insects. The pure parental lines simply need to be planted side by side in the field, crossing between the two being ensured by breeding self-sterility into the parents. It is even possible, where such self-sterility is not complete, to arrange, through a little genetic manipulation, that any plants resulting from self-fertilization – including brother-sister mating – are different in appearance from the rest (paler, say, or taller), so that they can be instantly spotted and weeded out.

Large numbers of F_1 hybrids have now been produced, not only among food crops but among ornamental plants, and fresh ones appear every year: petunias in dazzling new colours, improved in size and shape and length of flowering; transformed antirrhinums such as the azalea-flowered 'Madam Butterfly' and its dwarfer look-alike 'Sweetheart'; dazzling African marigolds such as 'Toreador' and 'First Lady'; sparkling F_1 'Carefree' geraniums (actually pelargoniums), smothered in bloom within four or five months from the date of sowing; vivid begonias such as 'Organdy' and 'Lucia'.

There is only one snag about F_1 hybrids. Many gardeners, out of a desire to improve their plants or simply to save money, like to save seed from particularly good specimens and sow it the following season instead of buying another packet. With ordinary varieties that makes perfectly good sense; indeed, it has long been the way in which improvements have been made to our cultivated plants. With F_1 hybrids, however, things are very different. If you attempt to sow seed saved from that first generation of uniformly excellent plants, you will find the results extremely disappointing. Instead of high quality, practically identical plants, the second generation will consist of a motley assortment of widely different and mostly inferior individuals. It takes great professional skill and high technology to keep the parent lines pure and to mate them correctly.

So far, most of the F_1 hybrids that have been developed and attracted the greatest publicity have been annuals. Now increasing use is being made of the same techniques to produce F_1 hybrid perennials – even shrubs and trees. There is the amazing F_1 hibiscus 'Southern Belle', for instance, with huge vivid flowers the size of soup plates: in spite of its tender, not to say tropical, appearance it can survive vicious frosts which would kill many apparently hardier things.

Sterile plants

Many of our most cherished garden hybrids – both F_1 varieties and ones more conventionally bred – are vegetable mules: strong, tough and handsome but unable to beget young. Their impotence may be due to a variety of causes. First, their reproductive organs – male, female or both – may be actually missing, having been bred out of existence. This is the common fate of many of the double flowers in our gardens, the extra petals being really transformed and aborted sexual parts. Secondly, the reproductive organs, though present, may have ceased to function: there may, for instance, be no pollen, or at any rate no fertile pollen, produced; or the ovary may be barren. Thirdly, even though the organs appear to function normally and produce seed, that seed may be lifeless. In such circumstances there is no hope whatever of propagating by sexual means. To attempt to do so would be as futile as putting a mule out to stud. Fortunately, though, sterile plants, unlike sterile animals, can be propagated by other methods.

In certain circumstances, where the failure of sexual reproduction arises from the fact that the cells contain the wrong number of chromosomes, fertility can sometimes even be restored by changing that number. This can be done either by happy chance, as in the case of that popular greenhouse plant *Primula* X *kewensis*, or by artificial means, in particular by the use of colchicine – a highly poisonous chemical extracted from the so-called autumn crocus, commonly known as naked ladies – which interferes with the process of cell division. This method is used increasingly by plant-breeders, not only to overcome sterility but to create bigger, and sometimes better, flowers, particularly among such luxury products as orchids.

Restoring sexual powers to sterile plants is, however, a job for specialists, and even they can claim only limited success. In the vast majority of cases alternative methods of propagation involve doing away with the sexual process altogether and raising new plants from bits of the old one, rather as if a new person were to be grown from the finger or toe of an existing one. Such asexual methods of propagation include taking cuttings, layering, grafting, budding, and multiplication by runners, bulblets and tubers. The latest technique is known as tissue culture: tiny pieces of plant are surgically removed, cut up into even tinier pieces under a microscope, carefully placed in vessels containing precise amounts of nutrient jelly made up to an exact chemical formula, and grown on under strictly controlled conditions of light, temperature and humidity in a laboratory as scrupulously germ-free as any premature baby unit in a maternity hospital.

Producing quantities of plants from pieces of the same original one is known as clonal propagation, and the group of plants so produced is known as a clone. The individual plants of a clone are of course identical in their genetic endowment, but what becomes of them later in life depends to a large extent on their upbringing. As with children, the treatment they receive helps determine whether they will be healthy or unhealthy, happy or unhappy.

Non-sterile plants

As well as plants that have lost the power of reproduction, a great many with their reproductive faculties intact are also propagated asexually. Often this is simply because such propagation is simpler, quicker, more reliable and/or cheaper than raising from seed.

With specially desirable cultivated varieties (called 'cultivars' for short), asexual methods have to be used almost always, even when they are more difficult and expensive. Indeed, where named clones are concerned any attempt at sexual reproduction is likely to be forbidden. When the name is protected under plant-breeders' rights, especially when it has been copyrighted, anyone attempting to sell sexually produced offspring under the same name as the parent could be in trouble. And if the cultivar concerned has been granted an award of merit or other distinction – which means that it can command a higher price – the awarding authority would have cause for complaint as well as the customer.

The reason is that the mixed, and often highly complicated, genetic make-up of most of our cultivated plants makes it impossible for them to breed true from seed. No seedling from the rose 'Peace' or from the apple 'Cox's Orange Pippin' could ever be exactly the same as the parent – and most such seedlings would be greatly inferior.

The different techniques

The many techniques of asexual propagation may generally be divided into two kinds: on the one hand new plants are raised from cuttings, layering and the like, where they are supported on their own roots; on the other hand they are produced by grafting or budding, where they are supported by the roots of another variety, another genus, or even another species.

Each technique has its advantages and disadvantages. Taking cuttings is perhaps the easiest method of raising plants asexually. Cuttings can often be rooted with great success by the amateur, and will grow into fine, healthy specimens with little or no trouble. But some are much harder to start, and need special nursing in an incubator unit if they are to survive, while others may start off easily enough but become difficult later, so that they need a period of weaning.

Propagation by the method called layering often occurs naturally: an ordinary shoot may have grown top-heavy and been bent down to the ground by its own weight, or a tree blown over so that a branch or a twig rests on the earth, and where the shoot or branch touches the soil roots appear. No doubt it was this that first gave people the idea of deliberately using the same method to propagate plants that cannot readily be raised from ordinary cuttings because they are unable to survive being rootless without support. Now millions of plants are raised by layering every year, both by professionals and by amateurs. Remember that the young plants will die if they are cut off from their parents too soon, before they are firmly rooted.

Details of how to bring plants into the world, whether by sexual or asexual means, are given in chapter 4.

CHAPTER TWO

Home or hospital?

ARGUMENTS RAGE over whether it is better to have babies at home or in hospital. Similar arguments apply to the question of whether it is better to raise plants yourself at home or get them when they are several weeks or months old from a nursery. Certainly there is a great thrill in watching a seedling emerge from seed you have sown yourself: there it is, a brand new individual with the potential to outshine all others and repay many times over all the love and care you put into bringing it into existence. And even if you raised it from a cutting, and therefore it is not a new individual, it can still be a credit to your skill and devotion, reminding you every time you see it of the friend from whose garden or home you got it. In deciding whether to raise a plant yourself at home or buy it from a nursery, you have to ask yourself whether you have the facilities, equipment, knowledge, and for that matter time, to give it at least as good a start in life as it would get from professional care.

Where hardy annuals are concerned, the answer is likely to be yes. They have a great deal of growing, developing and maturing to pack into a very short life, and even the slightest hold-up during their early days can seriously affect their future. The damage to fine hair-roots that is bound to occur during even the most careful transplanting may well give them a set-back from which they will never fully recover. So if you are tempted by a box of splendid-looking seedlings on a market stall, miles ahead of anything you could manage to raise yourself, think before you fall for them. Not only will they suffer severely from uprooting, but if, as is likely, they have been given a certain amount of heat to bring them on faster so as to catch the eye of potential buyers, they may not have been hardened off properly and so suffer also from chill. So a packet of seed, as well as being cheaper, may actually give better and quicker results than a batch of plants bought at the same time.

Hardy perennials are also on the whole cheap and easy to raise from seed, and need no protection or special equipment. Some of them, though, can be reluctant to germinate, and may have to be coaxed by one of the methods described on page 50. Though it might be ideal to sow them where they are to live permanently, and so avoid any root disturbance, usually they do not make much of a show till the second year, and would simply take up space, look dull, and need careful weeding. They are therefore usually transplanted into their final quarters in the autumn or early spring after they have grown for a season. Plants grown in pots or other containers will suffer less root disturbance, but this is not quite so important as with annuals, because perennials tend to spread, new roots forming at the outside of the clump while the old ones in the middle die away.

There is therefore not the same objection to buying hardy perennials from a nursery or garden centre. And, though you always stand a chance, however remote, of raising an outstanding new variety from seed, the vast majority of your seedlings will not be as good as the best existing ones. Most nurserymen, therefore, will take no chances with seed but will concentrate on a limited number of vegetatively propagated named varieties of proved excellence; since you will buy these in the dormant season, when you cannot see what they will look like, intelligent nurserymen label the plants with coloured illustrations showing (with perhaps some exaggeration) what they will look like in full bloom.

With trees and shrubs it is the same story: raising your own from seed is cheaper (provided that you can get the seed to come up), and gives a slim but exciting chance of producing something new, but it is more likely to produce inferior specimens to those you would buy. If you prefer to propagate from existing varieties, and can get a supply of the right material, you can try any of the vegetative methods described on page 59; but all these take time, and some take considerable skill and expensive equipment.

The same considerations apply to half-hardy plants. Some – particularly the annuals – are quite easy, provided you can give them the warmth and protection they need, particularly in their first days of life; some are fiendishly difficult; and some, especially named varieties which can only be propagated by vegetative means and the use of space-age technology, are impossible except by investment of time, money and effort in equipment, experience and knowledge.

In every case, you have to weigh up the advantages and disadvantages of raising the young plant yourself at home or buying one raised by someone else. Where hardy annuals are concerned the obvious course is to grow them yourself; with other plants things are not quite so simple.

A packet of seeds of a half-hardy annual, for instance, may seem very cheap, even in these inflationary times. When you work out the cost of providing them with the warmth and protection – not to mention the time and devotion – necessary to bring them into growth, you may well find that the bought plants are actually cheaper. Also, if you buy from a reputable firm, the bought plants are often stronger and healthier than anything you can produce yourself. The nurseryman can dispose of his handicapped or less-than-perfect youngsters without sentiment or compunction, so that you have only the best to choose from; whereas a great many people put up with miserable plants that they would not dream of buying, simply because they raised them themselves.

Where other forms of propagation are concerned – particularly when you come to such sophisticated methods as grafting and budding, not to mention modern scientific techniques such as tissue culture – the balance shifts more and more in favour of buying from the professionals rather than attempting to raise your own plants.

Health is an important consideration. The modern plant nursery is a place of strict hygiene, and the plants it produces have to conform to a high standard of health. Control of diseases, and of the pests that often carry those diseases, is in many cases automatic. And if plants do become infected, they can be quickly removed and destroyed. In comparison, the average garden is a throwback to the dark ages, full of disease and decay. That is why so often a young plant that was perfectly healthy when it left the nursery soon falls a victim to illness when it is taken home.

With many plants, inspectors visit commercial establishments to make sure that the stock is healthy and that anything falling below standard is promptly removed and burnt. This applies particularly to soft fruit such as strawberries, which unless constantly inspected for diseased specimens can deteriorate rapidly. That is why the sensible amateur, like the professional, will every so often replace his existing plants with certified disease-free stock raised by a specialist.

CHAPTER THREE

Preparations

PREPARING THE GROUND

THE NURSERY in which most plants grow up consists largely of soil. In order to ensure that it is in the best possible condition for their well-being it is necessary to know something of its nature and composition. A large proportion of most soils consists of particles of rock of various sizes, ranging from very fine ones, which form clay, to very coarse ones, which form gravel or sand. Where the finest particles preponderate the soil is referred to as a clay soil, and where, at the other extreme, the coarse particles preponderate it is referred to as a sandy or gravelly soil.

Each has it advantages and disadvantages. A clay soil is rich in minerals dissolved in the soil water, providing food for the plant roots to take in. On the other hand, because the clay particles are so fine they tend to cling tightly together, which means that the soil is sticky and difficult to cultivate in wet weather, and hard and even more difficult to cultivate in dry weather. A sandy soil is very easy to cultivate because the coarse particles drain quickly and do not cling together. On the other hand, this rapid drainage tends to wash away plant foods, so that plants growing in it may become starved. It is clear, therefore, that a good soil will contain a fair mixture of fine, intermediate and coarse particles.

Other important constituents of good soil are water and air, without which plants cannot survive. Clay soil tends to hold on to water but exclude air, while gravelly soil tends to lose water rapidly but hold a considerable amount of air. Yet again it seems that a balanced mixture of particle sizes in the soil is ideal.

There is another constituent of good soil which is very important for fertility, and which can do more perhaps to bring about improvement than anything else. That constituent is organic matter — some of it living organisms, including earthworms, bacteria and tiny fungi, but most of it formed from the remains of plants. In natural conditions these remains come from fallen leaves and dead stems and roots which have simply decayed on the spot where they fell and died. In gardens, however, it is much more efficient, as well as being tidier and more hygienic, to put such remains on a compost heap. After a few months they will have rotted down into an excellent soil conditioner, blackish brown in colour, crumbly and moist, sponge-like in its ability to hold water and release it as required by roots; it is also rich in plant foods released by the decomposition process. How to make compost is described below, but first let us look briefly at the question that has been argued over by gardeners for some time now: is it best for growing plants to dig the compost into the ground or to spread it over the surface?

To dig or not to dig?

Until recently it has been accepted without question that digging is essential to provide plants with the best possible environment in which to grow. The hard-packed soil was turned over in the autumn, left rough through the winter for the frost to break it down, then raked to a fine surface the following spring. Not only would the ground be improved by aeration but during the digging compost, manure and even weeds could be turned under and buried so that they would decompose faster, thus releasing food for the plant roots. These in turn were able to penetrate more deeply because of the loosening of the soil. Many people have now started to question this conventional wisdom; they point out that if the finely raked surface of the bare earth is beaten down by rain its structure is destroyed and a hard cap is formed which seedlings find very hard to break through; that in nature fallen leaves and other decaying vegetable matter are not dug in but lie on the surface. They believe that compost, leafmould and similar vegetable material should be spread on the ground, either as a mulch between plants or as a surface for sowing seeds. Certainly such a covering will never get beaten down hard by rain or form a cap when it dries – and if the layer is thick enough it may suppress annual weeds, or at least make them easier to pull out.

Most people, however, find the no-digging claims not sufficiently proved and continue to dig their ground, incorporating into it compost, manure or any other decayed organic matter in an attempt to achieve that ideal blend of clay, sand, vegetable fibre and rich brown humus that gardeners call loam.

How to make garden compost

First, it must be pointed out that garden compost is not the same as the sowing and potting composts described in the chapter on potting (pages 73–83), which are sterilized, and designed for plants in containers. Garden compost is made to be used in the open ground. It could in time be made from anything, animal or vegetable, that has at some time been alive, but the sort of material generally used is that which is soft enough to rot down within a few months: garden waste such as leaves, grass mowings, old flower heads and weeds, mixed with kitchen waste such as vegetable trimmings, tea leaves and coffee grounds. Some people use old newspapers, which is perfectly successful so long as they constitute no more than about a tenth of the whole and are well soaked in water beforehand. Manure may also be added.

Place the waste material on the bare earth – to allow soil bacteria, fungi and earthworms to invade it – in a stack about 2 feet (60 cm) square and 6 inches (15 cm) deep. You can sprinkle this with a proprietary activator to help speed things up if you wish, or sulphate of ammonia will do, since the purpose of the activator is to add a nitrogenous substance to aid bacterial action. A sprinkling of soil may be put over this first layer, to add more bacteria, then another 6 inches (15 cm) of waste material, then more activator, more soil and so on, till the heap is 4 or 5 feet (1.2–1.5 m) high. To conserve heat, you can cover the completed heap with plastic sheeting. Within a week, as the bacteria get to work, the temperature inside the heap should have risen to somewhere around 150°F (65°C), hot enough to kill weed seeds and most harmful organisms, and too hot for your hand. After a few days the heat will start to fall; some people then turn the heap sides to middle to make sure that all the waste gets equal treatment. In three months or so, according to the time of year, the compost should be mature and ready for use. Tidier and more effective than an open heap is a compost bin. There are several brands of ready-made compost bins on the market at a fairly modest price.

EQUIPMENT

There are really very few essential items of equipment that you need to enable you to look after your plants properly. First we must put a watering can, since all who have plants in their care need one, even if they have no garden at all but only a pot-plant or two in a bedsit. For outdoor use the best are probably those made of plastic and holding about 2 gallons (9 litres); they are light and easy to clean, which is very important if you have had chemicals in them. If you use weedkiller, which can cause serious trouble if traces are left behind, it is best to have a special watering can for it. For preference buy a can with a spout that has two detachable roses, a coarse one for general purposes and a fine one for watering seed-boxes. There is also a useful attachment called a dribble-bar, which is a perforated length of tubing that can be fixed at right angles to the spout; when held close to the ground it will deliver liquid fertilizer or weedkiller at just the correct rate as you walk with the can at a steady pace. For indoor use a smaller can is more suitable; there is no need for a rose since you will only be directing the water into the pot.

Next come those two essentials in the garden, a spade and a fork. They are going to do some hard work, so they must be strong enough not to snap, especially at the junction with the shaft. If you can possibly afford it get stainless steel ones, which are much lighter and easier to use since the earth does not cling to them so much. Next comes a hoe: there are many different patterns, but the most serviceable one for general use is the Dutch type, which is used with a pushing action just below the surface of the ground, where it cuts weeds off at the stem, leaving them to die. Once again a stainless steel blade is well worth the extra cost. A rake is essential if you are going to sow seeds in the usual way, both to get a tilth on the ground and to give a light raking after sowing to anchor the seed. Always leave the teeth pointing downwards, by the way, if you lay it on the ground: the oft-repeated joke about treading on the teeth of the rake is not so funny when the handle comes up and hits you in the face. A good pair of secateurs is a must if you are going to do much pruning; the best kind is a pair that cuts with a slicing action, and once again a stainless blade is a pleasure to use. A pocket knife is useful on occasions for paring large cuts to a smooth surface and for trimming jagged edges;

avoid those gimmicky kinds with lots of folding blades: one good blade is quite enough. The last essential, if you have a garden of any size, is a wheelbarrow, to enable you to shift earth and other heavy things without risking a hernia. A metal one with a single wheel will serve you well, but do not choose a big one in the hope that by saving on the number of journeys it will also save you work: a large barrow when full is not only an effort to push but might make a rut – or even get stuck.

A sprayer is a modern necessity. Inexpensive kinds are available with a pump to bring them to pressure and an adjustable nozzle to give a coarse or fine spray.

Toys

There are all kinds of other shiny and beguiling things on sale in garden centres and shops. Some of them, such as trowels and hoses and mowers, may be essentials or near essentials to you, depending on the size and character of your garden.

There are, however, increasing numbers of new gadgets, often quite pricy, that appear on the counters and shelves every week to tempt the unwary shopper. They should perhaps be called toys, and, like many of the pricy toys given to children which are really bought for the gratification of the parents, they may be simply a substitute for the attention that the ostensible beneficiary really needs to be given. Many of the gadgets offered – automatic devices for watering, feeding, ventilating and doing everything a plant could need – seem really designed to leave the plant all by itself. Not only does that rob you of the pleasure of looking after its needs and the interest of watching its progress, but it may be robbing the plant of the love and attention that it really wants.

CHAPTER FOUR

The new arrival

A SEED IS rather like an egg, containing both the embryo and usually a store of food (equivalent to the yolk) for it to live on during its development. The difference between the two is that the young of egg-laying creatures normally grow inside the shell till they are developed enough to be able to break out by their own exertions, while the embryo inside a seed remains more or less undeveloped. Outside forces are needed to enable it to break through the seed-coat; only then does it begin to grow and to develop into its different parts.

ENCOURAGING GERMINATION

The two outside forces that start the process are water and warmth. (That is why seeds should always be stored in a cool, dry place, so that there is no risk of growth processes beginning in the packet.) Through a tiny pore in its outer coat, the seed sucks in water till it becomes so swollen that the coat bursts, allowing the embryo to start into growth. A built-in mechanism usually prevents water from being taken in if the temperature is below a certain point. This protects the embryo from being stimulated into growth and breaking out of its protective covering when the soil is too cold; otherwise seeds lying in the wet earth would start to sprout during the winter: the water they had taken in would freeze during an icy spell, killing or seriously injuring the embryo by bursting its tissues.

Seeds of tropical plants which never experience cold in their natural environment may not have developed this self-protection against taking in water at low temperatures. In that case, they will be doubly at risk from a combination of wet and cold: not only will they be unable to resist liquid forced upon them but their prematurely emerging roots, designed for warmth, will be unsuited to cold soil and will probably be killed.

Many seeds have a built-in protective device that guards them against germinating when the weather is too hot. The seed is thus prevented from sprouting at times when there is a risk that the soil might dry out. Many species depend upon this device to protect them from the fate suffered by the seeds that fell upon stony ground in the parable of the sower: '*And when the sun was up, they were scorched; and because they had no root, they withered away.*'

The temperature at which germination is prevented varies from species to species, no doubt in response to the different conditions they have encountered in the course of evolution. A large number of quite dissimilar species show a sharp decline in their ability to germinate when the temperature goes much above 80°F (27°C). Naturally it is the shallow-rooting plants that suffer most when the top layers of soil become heated by the sun and lose their moisture; those species that send down deeper roots into the cooler and moister layers below do not have the same problem.

Since the short-lived plants tend to have shallower roots than the long-lived ones, annuals are on the whole more likely than perennials to have developed a protective mechanism that prevents germination at high temperatures. Seeds of the annual delphinium, for example, germinate very poorly, if at all, if the temperature is above 70°F (21°C), while those of the perennial species germinate quite happily at higher temperatures still. It is possible, however, to persuade annual delphinium seeds to sprout even during warm weather if you pre-treat them for two weeks before sowing by placing them on moist blotting paper (damp newspaper will do) and keeping them at a temperature of 50°F (10°C). By the end of the two weeks most of the seeds will have split, and some will have started to germinate; it is absolutely vital, therefore, that they should not be allowed to dry out, or they will shrivel and die in infancy. The same applies with even greater force to the planting of the pre-treated seed when its two cool weeks are over: the soil or compost into which the treated seeds are sown must contain as much moisture as they have become used to during their conditioning, and that moisture must be kept replenished by watering if there is any risk of drying out in the warmer conditions to which they must now become accustomed.

Commercial raisers of plants can use air conditioning to provide the cool conditions necessary for pre-treatment, and so keep up supplies of seedlings of difficult plants during spells when the temperature is unfavourable. Amateurs cannot usually manage things so easily. A cool cellar suitable for storing wine is ideal, but few modern houses have such things. The cupboard under the stairs might do quite well, so long as it has not got hot water pipes running through it. Even a domestic refrigerator can be quite successful, so long as the ordinary part is used, not the freezing compartment; the temperature will be several degrees below the ideal for such subjects as annual delphiniums, but even so a good proportion of the seed should come up successfully during the time of year when without cool treatment it would not germinate at all.

It should be added, however, that where hardy plants are concerned – whether annual or perennial – it ought not to be necessary to provide cold, or for that matter hot, conditions by artificial means; not only will time, trouble and expense be saved by sowing them when the natural temperature is right, but the resulting plants are likely to be stronger and better.

THE NEEDS OF THE YOUNG PLANT

It is a well-established fact that conditions at and immediately after birth are of vital importance in shaping a baby's whole future. The same applies to young plants. Perhaps it is going a bit far to think of them as having human emotions, but gardeners know exactly what they mean when they talk about their young plants being happy or miserable. If they are to thrive they need warmth, but not so much as to cause distress. They must be protected against drying out – though nothing makes the normal plant more unhappy than being constantly wet: not only does continual immersion in water drown emerging roots and prevent them from breathing but it is likely to lead to infection by disease germs, which flourish in wet conditions and may cause rotting and death. Fuller details are given in the section on watering (see pages 133–6).

Two other essentials are adequate feeding, but not too much, and the correct amount of sleep. So important is it to get these two requirements right that they are given a whole chapter to themselves (see pages 117–51).

Perhaps the most vital need of all in the early stages of life is a good supply of air. If the supply of oxygen is deficient for any length of time development may be seriously retarded, and the young plant may start life as severely damaged as any handicapped child. Many people are unaware of this need, because they have been taught that plants have the ability to use the energy of sunlight, through the chlorophyll which gives leaves their green colour, to take in carbon dioxide from the air and give out oxygen. Popular natural history stresses the fact that animal life too depends on this process, because the oxygen from the plants is breathed in by the animals, who then breathe out carbon dioxide; in their turn the plants transform that carbon dioxide into oxygen, and so the cycle of life goes on, animals and plants each giving what the other needs and taking what the other gives.

That picture is a bit too simple, though. Plants also have to breathe, and when they breathe they take in oxygen and give off carbon dioxide. During the day, when there is good light and they have plenty of healthy green leaves, the opposite process wins, and they produce by photosynthesis far more oxygen than they consume by breathing. But at night, when there is too little light for photosynthesis, the leaves use up oxygen from the air and give out carbon dioxide (which is why some people object to having plants in the bedroom).

For roots, hidden as they are in the dark beneath the soil, it is always night, and they need a good supply of oxygen to breathe all the time; as they never photosynthesize, they do not provide any oxygen themselves but need it from an outside source. (True, a few specialized plants such as certain orchids have aerial roots adapted to light, some of which even turn green and do their share of photosynthesis; but these are the exceptions, and need not detain us here.) So to give the roots what they need, the soil must always be of such a texture as to allow free access of air, as explained in chapter 3.

But it is not only when the roots have already grown that oxygen in the soil is so important. It is even more important in the vital first days in a new plant's life, before the roots have even formed; at that stage the young plant is having to live on its own substance, out of which it has to manufacture roots as soon as possible, so that it can start taking in food from outside before it uses up all its own reserves – in which case it will have nothing left to live on and will shrivel and die. To bring about the changes necessary to produce roots requires a good deal of energy, and this calls for an extra supply of oxygen. That is true for all new young plants in the process of putting down roots, whether they start from seeds, cuttings, bulbs, corms or tubers. We will deal with all these in turn a little later, but first we must deal with a subject as important and potentially troublesome to plants as it is to babies: the disposal of waste matter.

Excretions and their disposal

All living things feed, whether they are plants or animals, and in so doing they are bound to produce waste matter which they have to eliminate in some way. Since plants do not take in solid matter they do not give it out either. The waste substances they produce during the process of digestion have to be eliminated to avoid self-poisoning, but the elimination takes place in less obvious ways than with animals. Toxic products are carried away through a system of conducting channels in the plant's tissues and deposited where there is little fear of their doing any harm. In trees and other woody plants such poisonous substances finish up largely in the bark, where they not only do no damage to the plant but may even afford some protection against attacks by pests. Many waste products in solution are excreted through the roots, which develop a remarkable ability to take in what they want and eject what they do not want. Such secretions may not only get rid of harmful substances but help to keep the roots of competitors from invading the plant's territory; if soil conditions are such that the exuded products cannot escape, though, a concentration can build up which may cause damage.

Much of the waste matter expelled by the young plant's roots is gas. As we have seen, during the process of breathing oxygen is taken in and carbon dioxide given out, but certain other gases are given out too. If the condition of the soil is such that the gas cannot get away freely, the roots can suffer great distress. You can help by making sure that the soil in which a plant is growing is open enough to allow the gas to escape. In particular the surface of the soil must be sufficiently open and porous to permit free interchange between the air and gases in the soil, otherwise there is a danger not only of poisoning but of suffocation. Nothing is worse than a hard, compacted surface, particularly of bare soil. What is more, such a condition tends always to get worse, because every time it rains (or water is applied from a can in the case of pot plants) the surface gets more beaten down, and when it dries out that surface can become like cast-iron. This not only prevents gases from getting in and out but also stops rain from penetrating the hard crust, so that the water either runs off or stands on the surface till sun and wind cause it to evaporate, and the roots receive no benefit from the rain. The soil then becomes parched, and if a drought follows which lasts any length of time cracks may appear in the ground, tearing apart some young roots near the surface, exposing others to the risk of drying out, and allowing much-needed water to escape as vapour through the cracks. Worse still, bare, caked earth, in addition to being too hard for many emerging plants to break through, lacks the springiness or 'bounce' to absorb the impact of a hammering by hail or heavy rain, and risks being pulverized and blown away by the wind; that is how soil erosion happens.

Soil covering

The way to avoid these problems is to provide plants with the right kind of covering. This protects them against getting too cold in chilly weather or too hot during heatwaves, against getting sodden when the weather is wet or dehydrated when it is dry. A good covering layer also suppresses weeds.

Among the commonly used materials for soil coverings are peat, grass cuttings, straw, shredded bark, spent hops and saw-dust. All of them are best if they are well rotted; fresh material may starve the soil by taking from it nitrogen which the tiny living organisms responsible for breaking the material down need in some quantity to enable them to carry out their work. If the material is not sufficiently rotted, a sprinkling of ammonium sulphate or sodium nitrate well watered-in may give the creatures the nitrogen they require in the form of convenience food and so save them the bother of raiding the soil to get it.

Probably the best form of soil covering, or 'mulch' as gardeners call it, is well-matured garden compost, which you can easily make yourself from waste stuff from your garden and your kitchen, as explained on page 29. If it is very lumpy you can rub it through a garden sieve, but whatever you do you must not make it too fine or you may create a dense blanket through which air cannot easily pass.

Naturally the bigger a plant has grown the thicker the mulch you can apply to the soil around it. In the early stages while they are still very small, plants should have only a light mulching, if any, or they may get smothered. Seeds sown in the open ground are not usually mulched at all at the time of sowing but given a light covering of soil, which is quite enough so long as there is sufficient moisture to bring about germination. If not you must either give the ground a thorough soaking, from a fine-rosed watering can, or rely on a good downpour of rain. A brief passing shower is not enough. The seed should be sown, as gardeners say, 'into moisture': that is, the earth below should be damp, otherwise germination may take place in the moistened surface layer and the young roots then find themselves emerging into dry, unwelcoming soil beneath.

If there is a drought after germination, the seedlings may be in danger of being cooked without some covering to protect them. A surface layer of *dry* soil can provide quite good protection so long as it does not form a hard skin; that is why constant watering is a bad thing, because it turns the surface into a paste which then bakes into a dense crust. In ground with this tendency to cake, a good way to prevent it from happening is to rake sharp sand or grit into the surface to keep the soil particles apart.

So far we have dealt with the light and airy types of covering suitable for young plants in the early stages of life. As they grow bigger and stronger some plants can do with a heavier covering. That popular and beautiful climber the clematis, for instance, loves more than anything else to have its roots in cool, moist soil, protected from the direct rays of the sun. Yet though its nether parts seek the darkness, all the rest of the plant, from the ground upwards, is perfectly happy to be in full light. Though a good layer of compost or any of the similar mulches mentioned above will do a good job in providing a cool, dark root-run, that may not be quite enough, especially if the clematis is grown against a wall, where the soil tends to dry out rapidly. In such circumstances, a covering of something heavier and more impervious than compost can provide much better conditions. Stone is ideal. A layer of ordinary pebbles – brought back, perhaps, from a day at the seaside and placed upon the ground round the stem – can transform a struggling clematis, too feeble to bear more than a few miserable flowers, into a robust specimen smothered with blossom. And even heavier and more substantial coverings have a part to play in improving growing conditions; many a vigorous wall shrub or climber owes its rude health to a paving stone or two laid on the soil to cover the spread of its roots.

Indeed, a paved terrace with plants growing in pockets of soil between the stones is, from the plants' point of view, nothing but a patch of ground mulched with stone, providing a sheltered existence for the roots and saving them from the stresses and strains that make life so trying in unprotected ground. In the same way, a rock garden or a walled bank with plants growing in the crevices, though its purpose may seem largely decorative, is in fact a highly efficient way of using the protective properties of stone to provide the roots with a perfect covering against the changes in temperature and moisture that they so much dislike.

How thick should the cover be? It is during the first few days and weeks of a plant's life that the answer to that question is of greatest importance. It needs plenty of air to help it root quickly, so from this point of view its covering should be as thin as possible. On the other hand, the covering should be deep enough to keep in moisture and give protection. This is true for all new plants, even those raised from cuttings, but it is particularly important for those grown from seed, and they are the ones we will deal with first.

Depth of sowing

A good general rule of thumb is to cover seeds to a depth of two or three times, and never more than four times, the size of the seeds themselves. Experiments have shown that seeds sown deeper than that are likely to be at a serious disadvantage. First, fewer of those sown deeply are likely to come up at all. That is why the results of sowing rows of vegetables in drills are so often patchy, some parts of the row coming up thickly while other parts are sparse, or even bare; it may well be that slightly heavier pressure at some points when drawing the drill – combined perhaps with irregularities in the soil level – have buried the seeds too far down at some stretches of the row. (That, by the way, is why newly dug ground will often produce a spectacular crop of weeds, from seeds that have lain, perhaps for years, too deep to germinate until brought to the surface by cultivation.)

Secondly, the rate of infant mortality among those that do succeed in germinating is much higher with deeply sown than with shallowly sown seed. This may be partly due to exhaustion of energy and food reserves through having to struggle up through too much soil, particularly if it is heavy; it may be partly caused by shortage of oxygen at the critical early stage; it may be that the weakened young growth is attacked by soil-borne fungus diseases during its battle upwards. Also, especially during the spring when most outdoor sowing is done, though the surface of the soil may be warmed by the early sun, as little as an inch or so further down the earth may still be uncomfortably cold; experiments have shown that with sweet corn sown in the open during late spring seeds planted 1 inch (2.5 cm) deep nearly all came up, while less than a quarter of those planted 4 inches (10 cm) deep did so.

With most seeds, however (the exceptions, which need light for germination, are dealt with in the next paragraph), the covering should be thick enough to anchor the seed firmly, so that it is not washed or blown away. Also, where the seed-coat is tough, the covering should be heavy enough to hold the seed down: the emerging seedling has to pull itself up, bent double, against the resistance of the covering, and can only straighten itself up by dragging itself out of the seed-coat, which is left behind in the soil. This process of beginning life bent double is known as the 'crook stage', and can be observed in onions and leeks; many vegetables usually started in pots, such as cucumbers and marrows or squashes, must have the seed planted deeply enough to ensure that the seed-coat remains below the surface. This is particularly important with tomatoes and their relatives peppers and aubergines, which if not sown deeply enough will take the line of least resistance and lift the seed-coat out of the soil, with the result that the seed-leaves have difficulty in pulling themselves out of the coat and may be distorted, so that the plant has a poor start in life.

As can be readily seen with really small seeds, measuring say 1/50 inch (0.5 mm), it is simply not practicable to use the rather glib principle of covering them to a depth of two or three times their own size. How on earth could you give them an exact covering of between 1/25 and 3/50 of an inch (1–1.5 mm)? If you attempted such a thing out of doors, not only would the seed-bed have to be as smooth and level as a billiards table but the covering would have to be sifted so finely that it would cake in the rain and bake in the sun. The best thing to do is to mix the tiny seeds with some sharp sand, scatter the mixture either in extremely shallow drills or on the surface, and rake it very gently. With seeds sown in pots or boxes, it is easy to press the surface of the compost down to make a smooth surface, sow the tiny seeds thinly and then scatter a thin dusting of sand over them. Another benefit of using sand to cover the seed is that you can always see which pots and boxes have been finished and so avoid the possibility of mistakenly covering the seed twice over, as can easily happen if you use compost for the covering.

When watering, use a can with a fine rose, and because even the best-made cans tend at the beginning and end of each stroke to dribble a stream of water with such force that it can wash out the seeds and their covering, it is always best to start each stroke well in front of the pot or box and finish well behind it; then the cascade at the beginning and end will fall where it can do no harm.

The influence of light

Most seeds germinate best in darkness, or at least semi-darkness, so a covering is necessary to exclude light. Several species, however, especially those with very small seeds, will not germinate successfully unless they are exposed to light; so if you cover them up you are going to be disappointed. Among the genera of which some, or all, of their species have light-stimulated seeds are those listed by seedsmen under the following names:

Ageratum	Exacum	Lychnis
Aquilegia	Fuchsia	Molucella
Arabis	Gerbera	Penstemon
Begonia	Gloxinia	Petunia
Calceolaria	Heuchera	Physalis
Chrysanthemum	Impatiens	Platycodon
Cineraria	Kalanchoe	Primula
Coreopsis	Leontopodium	Saintpaulia
Doronicum	Linaria	Streptocarpus

Unfortunately there is quite a lot still to be discovered about the often complicated interactions between light and other factors affecting germination. The seeds of some plants become light-sensitive only after they have taken in water. In some cases freshly gathered seed may be stimulated to germinate by light, and in others inhibited; after a period of dry storage, the same seeds may completely change in their reaction to light. Very few seed packets carry any information on the light requirements of their contents (except occasionally in the well-known case of primula). If you are in doubt, the best thing is to press the seed gently into the surface of the sowing compost and then cover half the surface with a thin sprinkling of sand. In that way you will be catering for either taste, and if the results for the two halves are significantly different you will be able to make a note of the treatment to be given next time you sow that particular seed. Besides, if the results are conclusive enough you may want to share them with other gardeners, and perhaps make yourself a little money, by reporting on your experiment for publication in one of the gardening magazines.

So much for the general principles of raising plants from seed. Here follow a few details of the different types of plants that can be raised in this way.

Hardy annuals

These are among the flowering plants that give the greatest display of colour and form for the least money. Though they last for only one season they are tough enough to survive the cold weather out of doors. The vast majority of gardeners sow them in the open during the spring, when the soil begins to warm up. You can get bigger, stronger, earlier-flowering, more prolific and longer-lasting plants, however, by sowing the hardiest kinds in late summer or early autumn before the soil has started to cool down. Some of the most popular flowers in this group are calendula (pot marigold), candytuft, cornflower, larkspur, nigella (love-in-a-mist) and scabious.

Before sowing hardy annuals, make sure the soil is well prepared and raked to a crumbly tilth. It should be moist but not wet, or germination may be prevented. Sow thinly, both because seed is expensive and because overcrowding in infancy can lead to weak, sickly plants.

Biennials

True biennials flower during their second season and then die. They include forget-me-not, honesty, Canterbury bells, Brompton stocks and mullein (verbascum). Many others are grown as biennials, including sweet William, wallflowers, Iceland poppy and double daisies. They may be raised from seed in a greenhouse, but young plants cosseted in this way tend not to grow into such sturdy specimens as those sown in the open, either in a seed-bed or in boxes, in the spring or early summer, and transplanted to their flowering quarters in the autumn, while the ground is still warm enough for the young plants to root themselves into their new quarters before the winter. Keep an eye on the plants for a few weeks after transplanting them, and if the ground becomes dry give them a good watering; do this in the morning, so that the leaves can dry off before nightfall.

Hardy perennials

You will find this large group of important plants coded with the letters HP on seed packets and in seedsmen's catalogues. They form the basis of the garden border, traditionally confined to herbaceous plants, but in the modern small garden often mixed with trees and shrubs, with perhaps a few annuals to fill in gaps. For the best forms, complete with fancy varietal names and perhaps the distinction of a First Class Certificate or an Award of Merit from the Royal Horticultural Society, or a medal from one of the specialist societies, plants must be bought (or cadged from friends who are lucky enough to possess them), but for ordinary varieties of hardy perennials – most of which have reached a high state of excellence through careful breeding and selection – the cheapest way is to raise them from packets of seeds.

Though it is perfectly possible to sow hardy perennials in their permanent place in the border, that would be doing things the hard way. It is better to sow them in boxes or pots of seed compost (see page 75) so that they get off to a flying start, with no competition from weeds or pests, with ideal conditions for early growth and with just the right amount of mild, easily assimilated food to keep them going till they can get on to something stronger. When they are large enough to handle (normally that means when they have one or two pairs of true leaves), the seedlings can be pricked out (see page 86) individually into pots of potting compost (see page 75) and left to grow in the open till the autumn, when they should be planted in the positions where you intend them to flower. The added advantage of this autumn transplanting is that any weed seeds in the ground will have come up during the summer and can be destroyed by hoeing or hand-pulling, so that the young plants have a clean, warm bed in which to settle down and become well established before winter.

Half-hardy annuals

The plants in this group are those which, though they will grow and flower quite happily out of doors during a typical British summer, come from species native to somewhat warmer countries. They need a longer growing period than our short frost-free season allows if they are to develop to the flowering stage, so they have to be sown early in the year in a heated greenhouse, or one of the small propagators now available, consisting of a seed-tray covered with a moulded plastic lid, giving sufficient height for the seedlings to develop. The most advanced are those with some form of electrical heating under the compost, but satisfactory results can be obtained with unheated ones placed on the window-sill in a reasonably warm room. Even an ordinary seed-tray covered with a sheet of glass or polythene will do; in the early stages direct sunlight should be excluded by covering the top with a sheet of newspaper, but this should be removed when the seedlings come up, or they will soon become weak, pallid and spindly. Small quantities of seed may be germinated successfully in a pot filled with seed compost and covered with a plastic bag.

For healthy and weed-free seedlings, use only sterilized and properly prepared seed compost (see page 77), and prick out the young plants before they become overcrowded. Most half-hardy annuals are best planted out in the garden in late spring, when there is little danger of really cold nights; though a few of the more tender kinds are best left until early summer, at any rate in cold districts. Details of when to sow and plant should be given on the seed packet (all reputable seedsmen give such information these days, together in many cases with the year when the seed was harvested and/or the latest date by which it should be sown), and these instructions should be carefully followed. Two or three weeks before the seedlings are planted out they should be hardened off by being placed in a cold frame, which in the absence of anything more sophisticated can be simply a box covered with a sheet of glass, left off during the day but replaced during cold nights or when there is a savage wind. If there is nothing like that available, the young plants may be put in a sheltered spot in the garden – in the angle of a wall, or beside a fence – and if frost is threatened covered at night with a plastic sheet, or even newspaper. Only give such protection if it is necessary; the idea is to harden the young plants, not to go on pampering them (see the section on weaning and hardening, page 167).

Some of the half-hardy subjects give a magnificent return in freedom of flowering and vividness of colour when planted in the front of the border or in special beds. A few of them are not really annuals but perennials, well able to stand the winter in the warmer countries where they originated but unable to survive the rigours of our climate; they are therefore mostly grown from seed every year and treated like annuals, though some, such as dahlias, can be lifted before hard frosts damage them and the tubers stored for the winter in a frost-proof place ready to be started into growth the following spring, while others, such as the ever-popular pelargonium (commonly called geranium) can be kept alive through the winter in a greenhouse – or even on a windowsill – from cuttings rooted in pots in the early autumn.

Though the term half-hardy is usually applied to plants grown for decorative purposes, it is the correct term too for those vegetables, such as tomatoes, peppers, aubergines, cucumbers and marrows, which originated in warm climates and have to be started in heat in a greenhouse, a propagating case or some similar protected environment (even at a pinch an airing cupboard, which gives just the right heat for germination). They may be sown in seed compost in just the same way as other half-hardy subjects; after germination they may be given a reduced temperature and plenty of light, otherwise they will grow weedy and feeble and need extra support – in short, instead of becoming sturdy and self-reliant they are likely to turn into chronic layabouts.

Greenhouse perennials and house-plants

These are plants grown for their decorative value that are normally too tender to be grown out of doors, though they may be put outside on warm days, and even left out all night in really hot weather (but be careful when bringing them back indoors to examine them carefully in case they have picked up any nasty bugs during their excursion into the open air; usually you can pick off the odd pest or two by hand, but if in doubt it may be best to spray with a suitable insecticide).

Nowadays you are likely to find very few seeds in a packet, even though the price you are charged for that packet may give you a shock. So treat those precious seeds with great care and respect. Space them evenly over the surface of the seed compost, water them carefully with a fine rose or spray, so that they do not get washed to one side, give them the recommended covering of sifted compost or sand, and follow the instructions on the packet as to temperature. To give the seeds the best chance of germinating, it is usually best to cover the pot or tray with glass or plastic covered with paper.

Trees and shrubs

Some non-hardy fruits may be grown for fun as house-plants, from the stones of avocados or dates, or from the pips of oranges or grapefruits, sown into pots of either seed compost or potting compost as soon as they have been taken from the fruit. You are highly unlikely to get fruit from them, and after three or four seasons – if they last that long – they are likely to have outgrown their quarters and become lanky and drawn, with too much bare stem and too few rather pallid leaves at the top. It is kindest then to dispose of them, while they can still provide a conversation piece with friends and before they get too ugly and pathetic.

But we are dealing here with hardy trees and shrubs which, if successfully raised from seed, can in due course be planted out of doors. Some people sow them in pots of compost and attempt to germinate them in warm, or at any rate protected, conditions. Such methods do not give the best chance of success, however, and often lead to total failure. One problem is that the seeds may take several months, or even a year or more, to germinate, and in that

47

time the pot of compost is almost certain to have deteriorated, lost its structure and probably become sour, so that germination is inhibited, or if it occurs the emerging seedling may find conditions so discouraging that it shows no will to survive.

Another difficulty is that during the time between germination and planting out the restricted room inside a pot or seed-tray may cripple the roots, causing them to form a tight knot, incapable when planted in the garden of sending out roots into the surrounding soil.

For these and other reasons it is considered better to sow the seeds in open ground, so that when the roots emerge they have unrestricted room in which to grow. True, when they are transplanted some of their roots will be damaged, and even torn away, but vigorous young roots soon heal and burst into new growth – and above all those roots will from their earliest days have acquired an outgoing disposition instead of the withdrawn habit that is so often the fate of pot-grown ones.

The best time to start to prepare the outdoor seed-bed is in the late autumn, when it should be dug to at least a full spade's depth and left rough throughout the winter, so that frost can get at it and break up the clods. While digging, incorporate plenty of peat, and if the soil is heavy add some sharp sand, or better still grit, to improve drainage and provide air-space for the young roots when they appear. It has been discovered that in most cases the growth of trees and shrubs is greatly helped by infection of the roots with soil-inhabiting fungi, in what is known as a 'mycorrhizal association', which seems to benefit both parties. There is still a good deal of mystery surrounding the whole affair, but what appears to happen is that the fungal strands act as additional roots, greatly increasing the amount of soil penetrated, and so taking up more nourishment, particularly phosphate, of which there is often a deficiency. An excellent source of these benign fungi is leafmould, so a good supply of this, well rotted down during the winter, should be forked into the bed before it is raked down into a rough tilth during early spring. Do not put in the seed yet; leave the bed for a few weeks so that any weed seeds in the ground or the leafmould can germinate; they can then be hoed off before the bed is raked to a final tilth ready for sowing.

Before that last raking, it is a good idea to sprinkle some superphosphate over the surface at the rate of 2 or 3oz a square yard (60–90g a square metre). Though friendly mycorrhizal fungi may be able to make up for any deficiency of phosphate, there is no point in stinting this first essential food for the successful rooting of new plants. Unlike some other fertilizers it cannot harm them even at this delicate stage, and they will not take up more than they can use for growth.

Rake the seed-bed level, and if it is dry water it through a fine rose, but whatever you do take care not to let it become water-logged. Then sow the seeds evenly over the surface. Large ones, such as those of horse chestnut or oak, may be spaced at about twelve to the square foot (900 sq cm); small ones, such as those of rhododendron, may be set as close as forty-eight to the square foot (900 sq cm); those of intermediate size may be sown at somewhere between those two rates. Press the seeds into the surface, and finish off with a covering of coarse sand, or better still grit. That will give the seeds the right conditions for germination, protect them, and prevent the moisture they need from evaporating; it will also make it easy for you to pull out any weeds that appear.

Even the hardiest trees and shrubs are often delicate during infancy, when they can be severely handicapped or even killed by weather conditions that will leave them completely unscathed a year or two later. The worst enemy is wind, which can be extremely cruel to young growth – and it is not only cold winds that do the damage, but warm, drying winds, which are quite capable of killing and maiming in a remarkably short time. So try to site the seed-bed where there is something like a hedge, some bushes, or a house or high wall to break the force of the wind. A low, solid wall or fence can be worse than useless, because strong gusts are likely to leap over it and create more turbulence and havoc than if it had not been there. If there is no suitable permanent protection, you can rig up an adequate windbreak with a row of pea-sticks or branch prunings stuck firmly into the ground, or with some small-mesh plastic screen, or even wire-netting; the idea is not to try to stop the wind – which would then probably cause the protective screen to come crashing down across the bed – but to slow it down to a less damaging speed.

The other great enemy of young plants is frost, of which the worst kind is what is known as radiation frost, brought about by clear skies, which cause what little heat the young growth pro-duces to vanish upwards into the air, since there is no cloud, or even mist, to act as a blanket. So on clear, cold nights when sharp radiation frosts threaten, it is a wise precaution to rig up some temporary covering as protection; sacking or even sheets of newspaper can act as surprisingly effective blankets.

Inducing germination

Many seeds have such hard coats that unless some form of assistance is given to enable the embryo inside to get out it may remain trapped, and if it stays so too long after its proper time it may die inside. The problem may arise because of the unnatural conditions in which the seed was harvested and stored. In natural circumstances it will not spend months in a packet, getting harder and drier, but will lie where it falls, exposed to the weather – or in some cases subjected to rather more strenuous treatment by animals or birds. In the absence of such natural influences to help things along, artificial methods may have to be used.

In the simplest cases, where in the wild the seed-coat would be subjected to freezing and thawing, wetting and drying, when germination time came along it would have been weakened enough to let in water and split open to allow the swelling embryo to emerge. In such cases the technique known as stratification may work perfectly well. The seed is mixed with damp peat, to which enough sand or grit has been added to prevent it from caking together; the exposure of the mixture to low temperatures not only brings about the required weakening of the hard shell but also causes changes in the embryo which may be necessary to persuade it that it has been through winter and can now start to grow. In the old days, nurserymen used to put the seeds out in the autumn, sandwiched between layers of moist sand, peat or soil (hence the name stratification) and leave them at the mercy of the weather throughout the winter till sowing time came. Nowadays the same results can be achieved by putting the mixture of seeds, damp peat and grit into a plastic bag and placing it in the coldest part of the refrigerator, next to the freezing compartment (but not in the freezer itself, which may be a bit too cold).

Several kinds of seeds with hard coats are in their natural conditions reliant for their dispersal on animals or birds, which swallow them (often inside the attractive fleshy fruit with which many of them are surrounded) and later excrete them in their

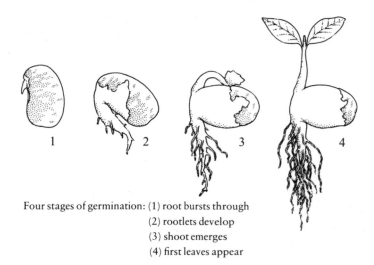

Four stages of germination: (1) root bursts through
(2) rootlets develop
(3) shoot emerges
(4) first leaves appear

droppings. To survive their passage, lasting perhaps several days, through the creature's digestive system, the seeds (often so hard that they are called 'stones') need tough protection, or they will themselves be digested. In fact that is the fate that befalls some of them, but the successful ones are able to survive all the hazards of their journey through the interior: heat, acid digestive juices, and the grinding and churning that goes on inside gizzards, stomachs and intestines. For these survivors, the hard coat has been scalded, corroded and ground till it has become thin and permeable enough to be capable of germination.

Artificial methods of dealing with hard seed-coats make use of the same conditions as inside the animal's gut: acidity, heat and abrasion. Commercial growers treat many kinds of difficult seed with concentrated acid, which eats away the outer coat. Timing is absolutely critical, however, because unless the process is halted at exactly the right moment the acid will attack the embryo inside and kill or maim it, so the use of acid is not recommended for the amateur.

Some seeds that have a particularly resistant waterproof coat can be successfully treated with hot water. Put the seeds in a shallow heatproof dish and pour over them water that has been allowed to cool down very slightly for a minute or so after reaching boiling point. Do not use too much water, or you may cook the seeds; use just the amount needed to cover them completely. It will cool down fairly quickly, but if all goes well it should take long enough to remove the coat's waterproofing. Keep the dish in a warm place for a day or two, and if the seeds are found to have swollen they may be sown. If they have not swollen, try repeating the hot-water treatment; that often succeeds after the first attempt has failed.

The most usual way to deal with hard-coated seeds is by some method of abrasion which breaks the smooth surface of the skin. Seeds large enough to be handled singly may be rubbed with a nail-file or nicked with a sharp knife or razor-blade till the embryo is exposed. There is no need to remove any of the coat; just break its surface sufficiently to allow water to get through; the resulting swelling will soon split the coat open. If you have difficulty in keeping hold of the smooth slippery seeds try holding them in a pair of tweezers.

With smaller seeds that are difficult to deal with individually, it is often possible to wear their hard coats down by the process known as scarification. This is done by rubbing them with some abrasive material. At one time the method commonly used was to shake them vigorously with sharp sand till their coats lost their shine, and this was done by commercial growers with various types of tumbling machine. Probably the easiest way for the amateur to scarify seeds is to line a screw-top jar with coarse sandpaper or emery paper, pour the seeds into it, screw on the lid and shake it for several minutes till the seed-coats are dulled and abraded enough to allow water to be drawn in.

Usually the taking up of water is enough to break the seed's dormancy, but sometimes the dormancy is complicated by the embryo's need for prolonged changes in its chemistry, often extending over two seasons, before it can be induced to sprout. In one such type of dormancy the seeds can be sown during spring in the usual way, without any special treatment, except perhaps for scarification if the coat is hard. During the first summer the roots emerge and develop underground, but there is no sign of any shoot appearing above ground. The bud that will grow into that shoot remains dormant until it has experienced the chilly winter temperature that it needs to break its dormancy and allow it to sprout. This type of dormancy is shown by the tree peony, or moutan, and by several species of viburnum; no doubt it was developed during the course of evolution in order to allow them to build up a good root system during their first season, so they would become firmly anchored before being called upon to send up shoots, which if they had been assailed by strong winds during the plant's early months could have been torn out of the ground.

Seeds of some kinds of plants show a variation of this behaviour known as *double dormancy*. Before being capable of germination, the seeds have to be subjected to low temperature. That brings about the changes necessary to enable them to send out roots when the soil warms up, and those roots grow during the summer, but no shoots appear. For that to happen, another cold spell is needed, followed by another period of high temperatures to force the shoots into growth. Commercial nurserymen may speed the process up by chilling the seed, then giving it a long enough period of warmth for the roots to grow, then subjecting it to a second spell of cold, and then repeating the period of warmth, creating within a few months two artificial winters and summers and so fooling the young plants into behaving in a very advanced way for their age. To use such artificial methods successfully, special equipment is necessary, together with exact timing. The non-professional, unable to create artificial seasons, has to wait patiently for nature to take its course.

The practical application of all this as far as the amateur is concerned is never to jump to the conclusion that all is lost simply because nothing appears to be happening during the first year, or even the second, after sowing. It is by no means unknown for the seeds of some species of trees and shrubs to lie in the ground for several years before showing signs of life.

Vegetables

Apart from a few permanent crops such as asparagus, nearly all vegetables are grown from seed. Since most kinds have a limited period in which to grow, a start may be made by sowing them as soon as the ground begins to warm up and become workable in spring, after the soil has been prepared as described in chapter 3. Some kinds of vegetable, such as broad beans and certain varieties of pea, are hardy enough in many areas to stand the winter out of doors after an autumn sowing and will give earlier pickings than those sown in the spring; but in very cold places there may be so many casualties because of winter rain and frost that it is simply not worth attempting autumn sowings. If you are in any doubt, ask for advice from your local horticultural society.

You can also get advice from them on what varieties do best in your locality. They will tend to be rather stick-in-the-mud in their loyalty to old-fashioned kinds – and that has its good side, since they are unlikely to fall too readily for the latest novelty, which may not live up to its publicity in your area, or indeed in any area. On the other hand, they may remain stubbornly wedded to varieties that were good in their day but are now hopelessly outclassed by superior modern ones, so be open-minded enough to try the occasional new kind which has received favourable reports in the gardening press.

The biggest mistake all too commonly made is to try to beat the season and get extra early crops by sowing before the weather is right, particularly while the ground is still too cold and wet. Some people seem to think that because only the hardiest can survive the cold such early sowing will somehow make them hardier, just as some of the ancients believed that exposing newborn babies to the cold night air would make the survivors stronger. In fact the opposite is true, for baby plants as for baby humans. Not only will a high proportion of seeds sown too early rot or fail to germinate, but those that do come up will be weakened, not strengthened, by the experience, so that those sown several weeks later in more comfortable conditions will very soon catch up and produce earlier, heavier and better crops. Follow exactly what it says on the packet about the right time to sow.

Some vegetables, such as lettuces, radishes and carrots, can be made to yield an early crop from a first sowing under the protection of cloches or polythene tunnels while the weather outside is still cold and miserable. However, many people make the mistake of sowing in cold soil and hoping that by covering afterwards with the cloches or tunnels everything will be all right. The correct thing to do is to cover the ground a week or two *before* sowing, so that it will have become warmer and more comfortable than the surrounding soil by the time the seeds are put in.

Even with crops that are not going to be given any protection after they have been sown, it is often possible to bring about an enormous improvement, especially in an unfavourable spring when the weather remains wet and cold, by covering the ground with plastic sheeting for a week or two before sowing.

There are almost as many old wives' tales about the raising of vegetables as there are about the raising of children. Many such stubbornly held beliefs have been tested over recent years by research workers at various scientific institutes. Often present-day methods of rearing have been shown to be misguided, while older practices, long abandoned as hopelessly out-of-date, have been proved to be superior. The traditional way of scattering seeds across fairly narrow beds, for instance, has been superseded in most modern gardens by straight, tidy, widely spaced single rows of vegetables with bare earth in between, making it impossible not to trample on the ground when sowing, weeding and gathering. Now, largely through the painstaking work of the National Vegetable Research Station (NVRS), the old ways have been demonstrated to have a great deal to be said for them, and knowledgeable people are turning back to them.

The truly up-to-date kitchen garden will have vegetables growing much closer together than recommended on seed packets and in most gardening books, and it will contain narrow beds, no more than 5 feet (1.5m) wide, with much less space between crops than we have become accustomed to, and with some salad crops such as lettuce and radish sown in broad-cast bands instead of rows.

Studies by the NVRS have shown beyond a doubt that closer spacing, though not producing such huge individual vegetables, can give a much increased crop of smaller – and more palatable – ones from the same area of ground. And, what is more, a good deal less work is involved. As the NVRS has shown, wide spacing might almost have been designed to make life easy for weeds, which have things all to themselves between the rows, with no competition from the crop, while in the rows the seedlings face competition not only from weeds but from each other. With closer and more even spacing, if weeds are dealt with early (no need to pull them up: they can be nipped off at that stage), the leaves of most crops will soon form a continuous canopy, giving weeds little or no chance. Wide strips of bare earth between rows also create the worst possible surface, liable to caking in the rain and hardening and cracking in dry weather.

Another fact proved by the NVRS is that attachments formed early in life are very powerful, and breaking them can lead to difficulties of adjustment and stunting of growth. The common practice of sowing members of the cabbage family in a seed-bed in the spring, uprooting them two or three months later and replanting them in new quarters, has been shown to give rise to much more disturbing consequences than had been fully realized. It has long been known that the wrench of being shifted from one place to another in many cases causes bolting, i.e. premature ageing, shown by running to seed before normal development is complete; it is suggested that sudden insecurity causes the immature plant to set about producing offspring quickly in case it should not survive. Now it is known that with even the most careful transplanting, followed by what appears to be satisfactory adjustment to its new place, the inevitable tearing away of much of the plant's root system may, even when growth seems to resume with little or no check, result later in an inability to develop a normal heart or head. This sometimes happens with cabbages, but it is prevalent with cauliflowers and broccoli, probably the most difficult for an amateur to grow successfully. Calabrese in particular is very sensitive to disturbance of its roots, which it is likely to repay by refusing to produce anything but miserable stringy little heads. Raising the plants in pots can improve matters, but even then a certain amount of disturbance will occur: besides, it may be hard for the roots to break the 'pot habit' of going round in circles.

The recommendation is that sowing should be made direct into the final quarters. Even if that means it will have to be delayed a few weeks, the plants will soon overtake transplanted ones and produce bigger, denser and more succulent heads. For those preferring the traditional white-headed cauliflowers, the NVRS has developed a technique of growing 'mini-cauliflowers' by sowing in close rows as little as 4 inches (10 cm) apart, a couple of seeds being placed together at intervals of 9 inches (22.5 cm) along the drill; or the rows can be 6 inches (15 cm) apart and the pairs of seeds also 6 inches (15 cm) apart, which will give just about the same number of plants per square foot (900 sq cm). Sowing in pairs allows for only half the seeds to germinate; if both come up, nip one off at an early stage. This method saves seed, saves weeding and saves space, giving a much bigger crop from the same area than the usual wide spacing – and because the plants mature much faster, they occupy the ground for a shorter time. True, the heads of mini-cauliflowers measure no more than 2 or 3 inches (5–7.5 cm) across, but there are far more of them, there is almost no waste, they can be frozen whole instead of having to be cut up, and they look much more appetizing on a plate, each nestling on its own surround of small leaves.

Fluid sowing

Extending the principle of starting vegetables in their final home and so avoiding the shock of being moved about, the NVRS has developed a technique called fluid sowing. This can be success-fully applied to such plants as tomatoes, which are usually raised in heat and not planted out till early summer, when the danger of frost is safely over. The first stage in the process is to start seeds into growth before they are put in the soil. Cover the bottom of a suitable plastic container such as a sandwich box with two or three layers of absorbent paper (tissues or soft loo paper are just right for the purpose), and cover this in turn with a piece of wet-strength paper towel. Damp this thoroughly with water, scatter seeds over the surface, and put the lid on the box to stop the moisture evaporating; if there is no lid, plastic film will do. Place the box in a warm, but not hot, place, say about 75°F (24°C). An airing cupboard should be satisfactory so long as the hot-water tank is well lagged. Within a few days the seeds will have sprouted roots, and when these are about ¼ inch (0.5 cm) long, sowing may be carried out. If this is not convenient the box can be put in a refrigerator (NOT the freezer part) for a few days, to stop the roots growing too long.

To begin sowing, pour water into the box to float the germin-ated seeds off the paper, then tip them gently into a fine strainer. The next thing is to mix up a sowing jelly. This can be bought specially formulated, but the cheapest and most easily obtained stuff for the purpose is cellulose paste sold for hanging wallpaper (not the kind with fungicide added). Use twice the amount of water it says on the packet, so as to make rather a sloppy paste; allow ¼ pint (150 ml) for 30 feet (9 m) of drill. Mix in the germinated seeds till they are evenly distributed throughout the paste. Now pour the mixture into an icing bag, and using a wide nozzle squeeze the contents out along the sowing drill just as if you were icing a cake. If you find it difficult to judge exactly how much pressure to use to lay ¼ pint (150 ml) jelly along 30 feet (9 m), make a few practice runs, using only the goo without the seeds. If you do not have an icing bag handy, an ordinary plastic bag with one corner cut off to form a nozzle will do perfectly well.

It is very important that the soil should be moist enough, otherwise the tiny roots will shrivel. After sowing, cover the seeds with soil immediately, to prevent them from drying out.

The sowing rate of ¼ pint (150 ml) to 30 feet (9 m) is just about right for most of the usual crops such as lettuce and onion; with more valuable seeds like tomato, where you get very few seeds in a packet, it is more economical to sow the jelly in blobs, each containing two or three seeds, at intervals of about a foot (30 cm). Tomatoes sown in this way in the first half of April will need the protection of cloches or tunnels for a few weeks, but those sown towards the end of the month need no protection; the risk is slight and late frosts usually cause very little damage.

Fluid sowing is not only, or even mainly, for somewhat tender plants such as tomatoes. It has proved extremely valuable for hardy vegetables as well, enabling the seeds to be germinated in controlled conditions so that they get off to a flying start. Fewer seeds are wasted, and after sowing they come up quicker and more evenly.

It may seem that if fluid sowing is so wonderful it contradicts what was said earlier about the bad effects of moving young plants. There is, however, one vital difference. With fluid sowing, the roots of the pre-germinated seeds have formed no attachments and so do not suffer the wounds of being parted. The whole technique of fluid sowing is described in a leaflet entitled 'Fluid Sowing of Pre-germinated Seeds', published by the NVRS as one of a series of practical guides under the general heading of 'Science in the Vegetable Garden'.

Other leaflets show in simple chart form low long it takes for a crop to be ready for use. Suppose, for instance, you want to find lettuce just right for gathering when you get back home from holiday on 17 August; you turn to the chart in the leaflet 'Lettuce Sowing', read off 17 August on one line, see where that hits the curve, and find that to meet that date you should sow on 28 June. Incidentally, the chart shows what we have already noticed, that it is no use trying to beat the seasons: lettuce sown in the open on 20 March is ready to cut a bare three days before that sown a whole month later – and, what is more, the later sown lettuce is much nicer to eat, because the quicker it grows the better it is.

VEGETATIVE PROPAGATION

We have dealt at some length with the raising of plants from seed because that is the only way in which new individuals can be brought into the world. All other ways of propagating plants, known as vegetative or asexual methods, merely consist of taking pieces off an existing plant and inducing them to lead a separate existence. Although the plant from which they have been taken is often referred to as the 'parent', that is really a misuse of the word. Parents and their offspring are quite different individuals, whereas pieces of the same plant, however far apart they may be growing, are really parts of one individual. So if you buy a 'Cox's Orange Pippin' apple tree from a nurseryman who propagated it from a graft four years ago, he will reasonably enough sell it to you as a four-year-old; but really, like all the other millions of trees of that name in existence, it is over 150 years old, dating back to 1825, when Mr Cox raised the original tree from a pip. And that, as we shall see, has a profound influence on growth, development and well-being. Old age brings infirmities and diseases, and it is often difficult, and sometimes impossible, to prevent these geriatric afflictions from spreading to all parts, including those taken for propagation, so that they start off with the same infection. Plants raised from seed, on the other hand, normally begin life full of youthful vigour and mercifully free from debilitating parental disorders. Still, if you want to produce exact replicas of some plant which you consider to be particularly desirable, vegetative propagation is the only method: there is, of course, no other way of reproducing sterile varieties.

Five methods of vegetative propagation are commonly used by gardeners and nurserymen. Starting with the most natural and finishing with the most artificial, they are: division, runners, layers, cuttings and grafting.

Division

This is the most commonly practised method of propagating herbaceous plants, that is to say those that die down to the ground in the winter. It is simply a speeding up of the natural process by which the oldest part in the middle of a clump becomes exhausted and eventually dies, leaving the thrusting young shoots at the edges of the clump to carry on and spread. You break the clump into pieces, throw away the worn-out middle (better still, chop it up and put it on the compost heap), and re-plant only the most vigorous outer portions. This job is usually carried out in the spring, when the ground is starting to warm up and new shoots and roots are beginning to form. It can also be done in the autumn while there is still some welcoming warmth in the ground.

If the clump can be pulled apart by hand, do so. That will keep damage to a minimum. Many tougher kinds, however, will not yield to such gentle methods. The simplest way to deal with them is to drive a fork through the middle and prise the clump apart. Many gardening books tell you to stick two forks, back to back, through the centre of the plant and by pulling on the handles lever it apart, but that is included really because it makes such a good illustration, since most gardeners have only one fork anyway.

Some plants, such as peonies and delphiniums, form hard, woody crowns which even a fork cannot easily penetrate. They may have to be cut through with a knife, or even a pruning saw, but if the tough old stuff is cut away the young outside pieces will usually soon recover from the surgery – always provided that you make quite sure they carry good undamaged buds to form new shoots.

Runners

This is the normal method of increase of some highly desirable plants such as strawberries (and unfortunately some highly unde-sirable ones such as that pernicious weed, the creeping buttercup). Where the runners touch the ground they form roots below and shoots above to make new plantlets. They can be helped in the process by being pegged down with hairpins – or pieces of wire bent to the same shape – into pots of soil, or better still potting compost (see page 75), sunk into the ground. The 'parent' plant from which the runners have come usually becomes senile and useless even quicker than the worn-out middle part of a her-baceous clump. That is why if you want the best strawberries you should never keep a plant for more than two, or at the very most three, years, replanting – preferably in a fresh bed – with the thrusting new plantlets formed on the runners; in a couple of years they too will be fit for the scrap-heap.

Pegging down runners

Layers

These are shoots normally growing more or less upright which have been bent down to the ground and caused to root at the point where they touch. Layering can occur naturally when wind, or sheer weight, brings down a branch or a shoot till it rests on the soil; if it is not too old and the conditions are right, it will respond to the contact by sending out what are known as adventitious roots (i.e. roots arising from parts where they do not normally form), giving the plant an extra source of food.

Many garden plants are increased by layering, which has the great advantage that the new plant-to-be still remains supported and nourished by the rest of the plant till it has become self-reliant and so can have its ties severed. Among the species and varieties commonly propagated in this way are border carnations. Stems chosen for the purpose must be non-flowering, or the attempt is unlikely to be successful. Make a slit through the stem at a joint, then bend it down and peg to the ground; many people dust the slit with a hormone rooting powder for quicker and more certain results. A small mound of good soil, sand or compost is placed over the pegged down joint and kept moist, but *not* soggy. If the operation is performed in early summer, the layered shoot should be sufficiently rooted by the autumn to be severed from the rest of the plant; after a few days to let it get used to being on its own, it can then be transplanted. If, like strawberry runners, it has been rooted into a pot, so much the better for its future, because its roots will suffer less disturbance. A good many trees and shrubs which rarely survive as cuttings may be layered successfully.

A special technique known as 'air-layering' may be used with subjects that are too inflexible to be bent down without breaking. In the days before plastic film had been invented, this was a very difficult and delicate process, involving cutting a clay flower-pot in half lengthwise without smashing it and binding the two halves, filled with a damp rooting medium, together round the stem, which had been wounded by cutting or slicing. Nowadays things are much easier, and thousands of shrubs and house-plants are propagated by the simple process of wounding the stem, dusting with rooting powder, wrapping with damp moss, covering with polythene film, binding with adhesive tape at both ends to stop moisture escaping, and then waiting for enough roots to form in the moss to make the layered plant self-supporting; the stem is then severed and the layer planted on its own. If you have a leggy rubber-plant in your home, with yards of bare stem and a bunch of leaves right at the top, try air-layering it in this way below those leaves; if it works you will have a much more attractive plant.

Cuttings

A great many plants are propagated in this way. Cuttings can be of three kinds: root cuttings, leaf cuttings and stem cuttings.

ROOT CUTTINGS

Comparatively few species are propagated from pieces of root, at any rate by the amateur. Among them are some trees such as poplar, *Catalpa*, *Paulownia*, and certain species of *Prunus*. Several herbaceous plants with fleshy roots can also be raised in this way, among them *Phlox* and *Gaillardia*. The pieces of root to be used are usually cut square across at the top end and obliquely at the bottom end, to make sure they are planted the right way up. The best time to obtain suitable roots is mid-winter with most species, when the plant is at its most dormant. The root cuttings, between 1 inch (2.5 cm) and about 4 inches (10 cm) long according

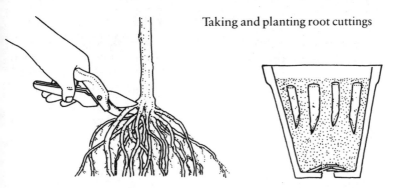
Taking and planting root cuttings

to kind, are planted in good soil or compost with plenty of sharp sand or Perlite to ensure a good air supply, and kept moist but not wet. If all goes well, buds will begin to sprout. If several appear, thin them so that they do not grow too crowded; if you are propagating a tree remove all shoots but one, or you will get a bush.

LEAF CUTTINGS

Only a few species can be propagated from leaf cuttings, but these include some very attractive house-plants. The well-known and well-loved African violet (*Saintpaulia*) is one. Take a leaf complete with its stalk, trim the end of the stalk neatly with a sharp knife or razor-blade, dip it in a little rooting powder and shake off the surplus. Now insert it in a pot of cutting or seed compost, gently firm the surface, water carefully, and place the pot in a propagator, if you have one; if not, create your own mini-propagator by putting a plastic bag over the top of the pot – blow it up to stop it from crumpling on to the leaf and secure it with a rubber band. If

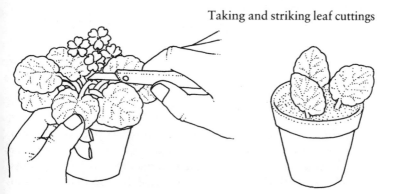
Taking and striking leaf cuttings

all goes well a tiny green blob will appear at the end of the stalk after three or four weeks, and as the blob grows bigger you will see that it is turning into a new plantlet. By the time this has reached an inch (2.5 cm) or so across, there will be enough roots to enable it to be transplanted to another pot filled with potting compost to provide the extra nourishment now needed for it to grow to full size. The original leaf should be cut carefully away, but be sure not to injure the new plantlet. If you wish, that same leaf can be used again to make yet another new plant.

Other members of the same family can also be propagated from leaf cuttings, notably that beautiful genus *Streptocarpus*, known as the Cape primrose (though it is no relation), modern hybrid strains of which make excellent house-plants, bearing throughout the summer a succession of foxglove-like flowers in a range of colours including blue, pink, purple, violet and white. In their case a somewhat different technique is used. Instead of being stuck into the compost by its stalk, the leaf is simply laid on the surface and pegged down, after first being scored with a sharp knife or razor blade across the veins on the underside; though results can be had without this slashing, there is no doubt that wounds greatly stimulate the process of regeneration.

Scoring and pegging down leaf

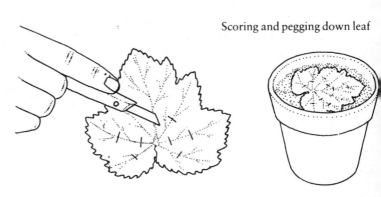

After being kept humid and warm for several weeks in a propagator with a cover to prevent evaporation (once again a pot with a polythene bag over it will do), the leaf will start to sprout little plantlets on its upper side above the places where the cuts were made, and when well rooted these can be detached and

64

potted separately. Exactly the same pegging-down method can be used to propagate varieties of *Begonia rex* and related species and their hybrids, with coloured, patterned and velvety leaves, known collectively as Rex begonias. It is best to use young leaves for the purpose, while they are still fairly small, because they will then be full of the vigour of growth; once they have reached full size they will be less ready to stir themselves into new growth. There is also the consideration that full-sized leaves are likely to be too large for anything but the biggest pots or other containers – though if only large leaves are available it is possible to cut them up carefully into small squares and use these instead of complete leaves.

An extremely important thing with all leaf cuttings is to make sure that the compost on which they are placed is moist enough to stimulate roots to form but not so wet as to discourage them. Plenty of sharp sand or grit in the compost will help to create the right conditions, particularly vital in the first weeks before the plantlets start to appear, because without any roots the leaf will rot if things are too wet or wither if they are too dry.

STEM CUTTINGS

Of all methods of vegetative propagation, the use of stem cuttings is the most popular and widely practised, both by amateurs and by professional nurserymen. According to the type of plant and the time of year, stem cuttings may be made from young growth, from mid-season growth in a semi-mature state, and from fully de-veloped end-of-season growth: the first are called soft cuttings, the second half-ripe cuttings and the third hardwood cuttings.

The soft ones are used mostly in the spring to propagate herbaceous plants, including chrysanthemums and dahlias; be-cause they are taken when the sap is beginning to rise and the days to lengthen, they root easily, grow fast and usually reach maturity soon enough to flower by the summer.

The half-ripe ones are taken in the summer mainly for prop-agating ornamental shrubs, of which a great many kinds respond readily to this type of treatment; they do not normally grow as fast as the first kind, and will not flower till the following year. In fact if any flowers do appear during the first year it is best to remove them; after their rootless start they need an undisturbed period for recovery and growth.

The third kind, hardwood cuttings, are taken mostly in the

autumn when the season's growth is over, to propagate some shrubs and such bush fruits as gooseberries and currants.

As a general rule, stem cuttings are severed just below a leaf, or, in the case of deciduous kinds taken after the leaves have fallen, just below a joint, where the tissue is solid right through, not hollow in the middle. There are two reasons for this: first, those are the parts where roots most readily form; second, there are no useless bits of stem left at the end, inviting rot, which can quickly spread to the rest of the cutting and cause decay.

Soft cuttings are the quickest to root, if they are looked after properly; unfortunately they are also the quickest to collapse and die if things go wrong. They need a closed environment, provided by a propagator of some kind, where they can find warmth and protection. As numerous infections lie in wait to attack the defenceless young, it is particularly important that sterilized soil should be used in the compost (see page 77), or alternatively rooting materials that are naturally sterile: a mixture made up of half peat and half sharp sand or Perlite gives excellent results, holding moisture well but at the same time draining perfectly.

When preparing the cuttings, make sure that they are sliced cleanly at the base; a razor-blade is better than a knife for the purpose because it can be drawn across the stem with a feather-light touch, so there is no risk of the crushing and bruising which can hardly be avoided if pressure is used. Dip the cuttings in a hormone rooting powder containing a fungicide to guard against rot, insert them in the compost as quickly as possible, so that they do not have time to wilt, firm the surface round them with your fingers (but do *not* ram it down, or you will prevent the free access of air, which is vital both to heal the wound and to stimulate root growth) and lose no time in placing them in the propagator. This should be kept closed for a few days, but when the cuttings perk up and show signs of new growth you can start giving a little ventilation; this should be increased till the cover can be removed without causing them to flag. Watch it, though: do not leave them with no protection against drying out until you can see that they are able to stand up for themselves.

Half-ripe cuttings are a good deal less likely to droop, because by the time they are taken they have acquired a certain amount of strength and can more or less hold themselves up. On the other hand they take considerably longer to root than soft ones do (maybe five weeks or more instead of two or three), and since they cannot show distress so obviously by simply flopping, they may look all right for a few weeks, so that you think they are doing well, and then suddenly dash your hopes by dropping all their leaves, and when you pull them up you find not the slightest sign of a root. If you take the cuttings at the right time, however, while they are still growing but beginning to harden, you should have a fair rate of success. A great deal depends on the vigour of the shoot; many nurserymen who raise numbers of plants from half-ripe cuttings make sure of a good supply of extra-vigorous material by pruning the shrubs intended for propagation right back as hard as they can, practically to ground level, in the dormant season, so that a thicket of new stems springs up when growth starts again. It is a highly successful way of getting plenty of good material for cuttings but rather unsightly in its results, and hardly to be recommended for a favourite shrub in your garden.

A very efficient method of dealing with cuttings of this type is the technique known as mist propagation. This makes use of special nozzles which give an extremely fine spray, and it works automatically by means of an 'artificial leaf', controlling an electrical circuit which switches the mist on or off according to the requirements of the cuttings. The success rate with this system is extremely high, but the technology (and the cost) involved make it more suitable for the professional than for all but the very keen amateur. Besides, after being reared in such scientifically controlled conditions, the cuttings need a period of rather specialized weaning before they are ready for normal life (see page 167).

Hardwood cuttings may wait several months before they root, but they have no problems of wilting or drooping, since being normally deciduous they will usually have lost their leaves by the time they are taken in the autumn. There is, however, no need to wait till every last leaf has dropped; the remainder will fall shortly after the cutting is made. If they are hardy they can be planted out of doors, where they need none of the protection given to soft and half-ripe cuttings; indeed, some people maintain that the more exposure they get to harsh weather conditions during their first winter the quicker and more vigorously they will produce both roots and shoots in the spring, because of the chemical changes brought about by frost. Some hormone rooting powders are available in a special grade for hardwood cuttings, stronger than the grades sold for soft and half-ripe ones. If your soil is heavy and apt to become sticky during the winter, it is a good idea to place some sand or grit round the base of the cuttings when putting them in the ground; a simple way to do this is to make a fairly shallow slit trench with a spade, sprinkle a good layer of sand or grit along the bottom, insert the cuttings, replace the soil round them and firm it down.

A few hardwood cuttings are taken of plants that are not hardy outside, and these of course have to be given the protection of a greenhouse or frame. While they remain leafless they lose little or no moisture to the air, so they do not have to be kept in a close, humid atmosphere like soft and half-ripe cuttings; and the compost must be watered very sparingly, since at first, and perhaps for several months, there will be no roots to draw in any surplus and no leaves to breathe it out.

Though hardwood cuttings must be fully ripened, they should only be made from stems that have grown during the current season; older wood simply has not the same power to regenerate. The same is true of varieties themselves; the older they are the more difficult it is to propagate from them. Take deciduous azaleas, for example: the magnificent old Ghent hybrids, with fragrant, honeysuckle-like flowers, originated from crosses made in Belgium about 150 years ago, and are much less easy to propagate than the comparatively youthful Knap Hill and Exbury hybrids, which go back only about forty years – and which are in their turn not so easy to multiply from cuttings as more recent crosses still. Though by modern scientific methods, using everything from surgery to courses of hormones, it is possible to force even some stubborn ancient hybrids into yielding material juvenile enough in its responses to propagate from, it appears that there is an age limit beyond which the life of an individual variety cannot usefully be prolonged.

Hardwood cuttings of deciduous plants have to live entirely on their own reserves till they start into growth. If those reserves are used up before growth begins, the cutting will simply die; and since the higher the temperature the faster the reserves are used up, that is one reason why hardwood cuttings should be kept as cool as possible.

Grafting

This is the most sophisticated method of propagation, and takes skill to perform. It consists essentially of uniting two different plants, one – known as the rootstock – providing the roots, and the other – known as the scion – providing the top growth. Basically there are two reasons for grafting. The first is to prop-agate plants which it is impossible, or difficult, or expensive, to get to produce roots themselves. The second is to regulate growth, so that if the scion variety is either too feeble or too coarse the rootstock will increase or reduce its exuberance, so that it grows the way you want it. In the case of fruit trees, roses and many other important subjects, grafting is done for both reasons at once. Most of the popular varieties are reluctant to root (though the nurserymen and scientists are working on it), but they can be grafted easily and successfully; also they grow in very different ways – some fast, some slow, some tall, some dwarf, some spreading, some dense – so if they were on their own roots the orchard or rose garden would soon be a shambles, with the aggressive ones grabbing more than their fair share of space and the shy ones not getting a look in.

Though the best known and most widely practised kinds of grafting involve the joining together of two woody stems, there are a few cases where the stem of the scion is grafted directly into the fleshy roots of the stock. This is the method mainly used by specialist nurserymen to propagate that spectacularly beautiful flowering shrub the tree peony or moutan; it needs great skill and experience, which is why tree peonies are not cheap. Because of the unusual method of grafting, if you get a tree peony to plant in your garden you must make the hole deep enough for the junction of scion and stock to come below the surface of the ground. Then the scion will make its own roots, and the stock (of a common herbaceous kind), having completed its job as nurse to the new plant, will no longer be needed.

Splice-grafting is one of the most commonly used methods of

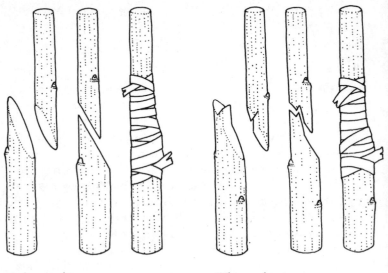

Splice grafting   Whip and tongue

grafting woody stems. It is suitable when the rootstock and scion, both one year old, are of more or less the same thickness. The rootstock plant has its top cut off, then the remaining stem is sliced obliquely upwards with a very sharp knife. A similar oblique slice is cut from the base of the scion, then the two cut surfaces are brought together in intimate contact and bound firmly with raffia or plastic tape so that they cannot move. The binding can be further covered with grafting wax or paint to stop the cut surfaces from losing moisture, but with securely bound plastic tape there is little fear of drying out nowadays.

As an added way of making the union of rootstock and scion closer and more stable, some people cut a nick downwards in the rootstock and upwards in the scion so that they can push one into the other in what is called a whip and tongue joint. Splice-grafting is usually performed in the spring, just as growth is starting, and success in the operation is increased if the scion has been retarded by being cut from its parent plant in late autumn and half buried in soil during the winter.

Budding, which is far the most widely used method of prop-

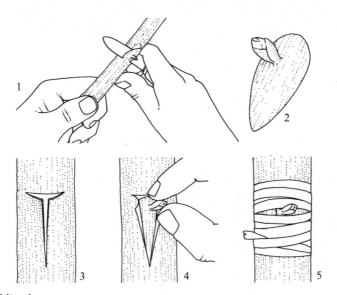

Budding by stages:
(1) slicing out the bud; (2) bud prepared; (3) T incision; (4) slipping in bud; (5) binding in

agating roses commercially, is usually carried out in the summer when the plants are in full growth. The scion in this case is not a complete piece of stem but a bud, attached to a shield-shaped piece of bark, sliced from a vigorous shoot. Two incisions at right angles are made in the stem of the rootstock so as to form a T; flaps of bark are gently raised on each side of the vertical cut, and the bud is carefully slid into place in the V-shaped aperture thus exposed. The flaps of bark are brought back into place, any surplus piece at the top of the scion is cut off flush with the horizontal incision of the T, and the job is completed by binding the bud securely in. If all goes well, the bud should start into growth the following spring. The stem of the rootstock should be cut cleanly off just above the bud so that all the rising sap will be concentrated into making it grow.

There are many other techniques of grafting, but the basic principles are the same as for the two methods just briefly described, and indeed as for every other method of vegetative propagation: use only young, vigorous and healthy material, whether it is roots, leaves or shoots.

CHAPTER FIVE

The potting routine

CORRECT POTTING consists of making conditions comfortable, avoiding undue wetness or dryness, and developing habits of scrupulous cleanliness.

WATERING

Quite early in the rearing of plants in pots and other containers – a practice that goes back to at least 3,000 years ago, when the Egyptians used container-grown plants to decorate their temples – it must have been noticed that constantly wet conditions were very harmful to growth; indeed, if prolonged, such conditions could lead to death. Since then every writer on gardening has stressed the fact that more plants are killed by too much watering than by too little. There seems to be a natural human tendency to give as much as possible to young things in one's care; to withhold seems rather mean. And since where young plants are concerned the easiest thing to give is water, the giving tends to be overdone. The result, of course, is spoiling.

The dangers of spoiling through excess have been stressed so much, however, that some owners of plants in pots have gone to the other extreme and given too little water. The effect is the same: roots shrivelled by excessive dryness are as incapable of taking in water properly as roots destroyed by drowning; the plant wilts, and if things are not remedied it dies of dehydration. And even if the plant can be rescued in time, it will probably remain sickly.

Modern techniques of automatic watering, developed by many commercial growers to cut down the labour costs involved in watering by hand, have to a large extent solved the problem, ensuring that the compost round the roots is neither too wet nor too dry. The amateur without such installations will have to continue with the routine developed by the nurseries in the days when labour was cheap: that is, he will have to go round daily inspecting the pot-plants individually, to make sure that they are not suffering from an excess of wetness or of dryness. For ways of judging whether a pot needs water see pages 133–6.

POTTING ON

The old-fashioned clay pots, filled with growing medium consisting wholly or mainly of earth, let out moisture rather readily. Evaporation through the pores of the pot wall could quite rapidly lead to dryness of the soil inside, not only on summer days when the sun's rays increased the rate of water loss but on cold nights, when as much – if not more – loss might be caused by the heating system in the greenhouse going at full blast to maintain the right temperature.

Naturally, the smaller the pot the quicker this danger point could be reached. It might seem that the simplest way to avoid the problem would be to use only large pots, so that the soil inside was not so subject to drying out. That is not the answer, however, especially where very young plants are concerned. In the enclosed environment of a pot, the delicate first roots simply do not have the power to suck up enough water from any considerable volume of soil to keep it from remaining too wet for too long after watering. To add to the problem, the bigger the pot the smaller the surface area of its wall is in relation to the contents, so evaporation through that wall is unlikely to be rapid or complete enough to compensate for the inability of the young plant to draw up and lose by transpiration more than a very limited amount of water.

Traditionally, then, the accepted thing to do was to start the young plants, either sown direct or pricked out from seed-trays, in the smallest containers available, known in the old days as 'thimbles' and measuring less than 2 inches (5 cm) across. When the roots had grown sufficiently to make their way through the soil to the wall of the pot, the plant was 'potted on' into the next size, known as a 'thumb pot' and measuring about 2½ inches (5 cm) across. Only when the roots had once again reached the side of the pot and grown around the soil enough to hold it together during transplanting was the plant transferred to the next size of pot, known as a 'sixty' and about 3 inches (7.5 cm) across. And so the process of potting went on: the next size up being 4½ inches (11 cm), then 6 inches (15 cm), 8½ inches (21 cm), 9½ inches (24 cm) and 11½ inches (29 cm), till a large specimen plant might finish up in a pot 18 inches (45 cm) across, or even more.

The important thing was that a plant should never be transferred at any stage into a pot more than one size bigger. It was a tedious process, partly designed no doubt to make sure that the garden boy was kept busy, but when conscientiously performed it gave excellent results. The reason was that at no time were roots required to face a large mass of extra soil beyond their capacity to cope; and by the time the larger pot sizes were reached the plant would be strong enough to draw in water quickly enough to compensate for the proportionately much reduced evaporative area of the pot wall.

The problem is that to manage such a system successfully, especially with the youngest plants in the smallest pots, there really needs to be someone present most of the time, to make sure that nothing is allowed to become too wet or too dry and to pot on as necessary. Even commercial nurseries nowadays find it so difficult to find, and afford, the necessary labour to keep such a system going that those who want to stay in business have had to turn to modern automatic methods. The ordinary amateur, who has to be away a good deal of the time, simply cannot give the constant attention that the old methods demand, so he must turn more and more to newer materials and techniques that make it possible to cut out much of the potting ritual without letting the well-being of the plants suffer.

SEED AND POTTING COMPOSTS

One of the most important steps forward in understanding the needs of plants in pots was the experimental work carried out at the John Innes Horticultural Institution in the 1930s. What triggered the experiments off was a calamity. In 1933, after large numbers of Chinese primulas had been successfully grown in pots at the Institution every season for the past twenty years, a mysterious wilt appeared and a high proportion of the plants suddenly collapsed and died. The most likely culprit seemed to be some sort of soil-borne disease, so the following year it was decided to tackle the problem by sterilizing the soil in which the primulas were grown. To everyone's dismay, that made matters worse: the rate of germination was seriously reduced, the seedlings grew badly, and to crown it all the wilt was not eliminated.

In trying to find out what had gone wrong, scientists at the Institution discovered to their surprise that no proper investigation had ever been made of the soil in which many thousands of pot-plants were grown there. What had been used until then were the old traditional potting mixtures, consisting mainly of earth with varying and somewhat haphazard amounts of leafmould and sand, sometimes with the addition of a whiff of manure, and perhaps the odd sprinkle of fertilizer as the plants grew bigger. Since the ingredients were so variable and no accurate measurements of the proportions of each were made, it was impossible to tell precisely what might have been responsible for failure – or for that matter success.

John Innes composts

To throw some much-needed light on the matter, a very thorough and careful series of experiments was conducted at the John Innes Institution over the next few years to establish once and for all what kind of compost could be relied upon to give plants the best possible start in life. The results of the experiments showed quite clearly that traditional methods had condemned countless numbers of pot-plants to a deprived childhood, from which many of them never recovered. The three commonest mistakes were poor physical conditions, faulty feeding and lack of precautions against infection by harmful organisms. Detailed study of these three critical factors led to the formulation of the John Innes composts, standardized and precisely proportioned mixtures designed to give optimum results every time.

The results of the investigation, together with full instructions for making up the new composts, were first published in 1939, in *Seed and Potting Composts*, which was an instant success.

The publication completely revolutionized methods of plant rearing. At first a few diehards resisted the new ways, protesting that plant nurture was an art, not a science, and that different plants had different needs which could only be met by individual concoctions of a somewhat mysterious nature. When, however, it became obvious that practically every species and variety of plant did much better in the new standardized composts, the diehards were soon silenced. Since then millions of tons of John Innes composts have been made and used, to the great benefit both of the plants and of their growers. In particular commercial nursery-men saw the advantages of the new mixtures, not only in the superiority but in the complete predictability of their perform-ance, and soon most of the leading professional growers were using nothing else.

There is no reason at all why the amateur cannot mix up his own John Innes composts, so long as he can find a reasonably simple and not too messy way of sterilizing the loam (gardeners' jargon for good top-soil) which forms the main ingredient. For small quantities the easiest method is to use a large saucepan. Put about ½ inch (1¼ cm) water in the bottom and then fill up loosely with *dust-dry* soil which has been sifted through a ¼ inch (5 mm) sieve to remove lumps and stones. Put the saucepan on the stove and turn up the heat till the water boils; then turn it down and leave it at simmering point for a quarter of an hour. Tip the soil out on to a clean surface and spread it out to allow excess moisture to evaporate. The whole process is as simple as boiling the baby's bottle to sterilize it, and the purpose is the same: to get rid of organisms, commonly called 'bugs', that are liable to attack in the vulnerable early stages of life. The temperature reached by the soil during sterilization is also high enough to kill all weed seeds, which used to be a great nuisance in the old days.

If you need more than a saucepanful of soil at a time, or if you or other members of the household object to the presence and smell of earth being heated in the home, there are several specially designed soil sterilizers on the market, of which the most con-venient and trouble-free are probably the electric ones. Before attempting to use such apparatus, which can be dangerous if wrongly handled, read the instructions from beginning to end, and follow them slavishly.

The two other main ingredients of John Innes composts are peat and sand. Because when bought from a reputable source these contain few if any harmful organisms they need not be sterilized; indeed, they *must not* be sterilized, particularly the peat, since the effects of doing so are highly detrimental to plant growth.

There are two different types of John Innes compost. The first is the seed compost (known in the trade as JIS), used for germinating seedlings and seeing them through their early days, and the second is the potting compost (known as JIP), providing a richer, more advanced diet for older and stronger plants, which need more varied food and more of it. The recipes that follow are the original ones formulated at the John Innes Institution after careful and painstaking experiments, and it is important that they should not be deviated from in any way.

John Innes Seed Compost
Sterilized loam	2 parts (by volume)
Peat	1 part
Sand	1 part

To each bushel (8 gallons/36 litres) add:
| Superphosphate | 1½ oz (43g) |
| Chalk | ¾ oz (22g) |

John Innes Potting Compost
Sterilized loam	7 parts
Peat	3 parts
Sand	2 parts

To each bushel (8 gallons/36 litres) add:
| JI Base | 4 oz (113g) |
| Chalk | ¾ oz (22g) |

The superphosphate should be ground into powder, not made into granules, since these cannot be incorporated uniformly throughout the compost. Suitable chalk may be bought as ground chalk, ground limestone, limestone flour or whiting. JI Base consists of 2 parts (by weight) of hoof and horn (⅛-inch (3mm) grist), 2 parts of superphosphate and 1 part of sulphate of potash. You can mix it up yourself from the separate ingredients, but there is really no point in doing so, since it will cost you little or no more to buy it ready mixed.

Since the quantities of fertilizer and chalk are very small compared with the rest of the components, it is not easy to incorporate them evenly throughout the compost so that every thimbleful contains its due share. The simplest way is to mix the fertilizer and chalk with the sand first; this can then be added to the loam and peat and stirred to make a homogeneous mixture.

There is no doubt that home-produced John Innes composts, when well made, provide an ideal environment for healthy and vigorous growth. The reason is that freshly mixed compost gives markedly better results; as compost gets older, chemical inter-action between the ingredients causes it to change for the worse. If you cannot face the fuss and bother of mixing your own, however, or you are too busy with other things, you can buy ready-made John Innes composts in plastic bags from your local garden centre or other horticultural supplier. Buy from a firm where business is brisk; then you are unlikely to find yourself landed with old stock, which may have been standing for months, or even years. And do not buy more than you can use within a few months.

Be careful to say whether you want seed or potting compost, and examine the label on the bag to make sure you get what you asked for.

When using the composts, it is important that *they should never be mixed together*. They have different functions to perform. As explained in chapter 8, plants in their earliest stages need a very mild diet; anything stronger may prevent seeds from germinating at all, or if they do germinate may severely damage the emerging roots. That is why a separate formula had to be devised for seeds (though it was later found to be admirable for striking cuttings, since their emerging roots are just as easily damaged as those of seedlings), with restricted food and a more open texture, to prevent the wetness that may cause trouble in the early days.

Though some people sow a few of the larger seeds (such as sweet peas) direct into the potting compost because of their more robust constitution and appetite even in infancy, all fine seeds (like those of begonia) and medium seeds (like those of nemesia) are best sown, and also pricked out, into the seed compost. As can be seen (page 207), normal good practice is to sow several seeds and then thin the resulting seedlings. However, people experienced in the ways of pot-plants have often remarked that if for some reason the thinning is delayed, the plants left to grow up together frequently thrive better than if they were isolated at an early age. The most practical explanation might be that (so long as the seedlings are not so overcrowded as to interfere with each other's growth) the companionship is beneficial because, with several developing root systems instead of one drawing in water, the compost is less likely to stay sodden after watering.

An additional benefit of the new composts has been that because of their scientifically established balance of ingredients, combining excellent moisture-holding capacity with good drainage, they provide a much more welcoming environment for new roots, without the dangers of waterlogging or drying out that existed with the old traditional mixtures. It is therefore no longer necessary as plants grow bigger to pot them on so often. Instead of always moving them into pots only one size bigger than their present ones, they can be put into pots two or three sizes bigger. And it is no longer necessary when potting on to ram the new compost round the old with a potting stick, as used to be the custom. Recent work carried out at the Crops Research Institute has shown that ramming is in fact harmful, because reasonably large pores in the compost are needed for healthy growth. Ideally some nine-tenths of the volume of the compost should consist of air space. Furthermore, if the pores are diminished in size by compression they cease to work properly; not only do small pores impede drainage, but they cling on to the water so tightly that the roots are unable to suck it in. A plant that is unable to obtain any more water is said to have reached its 'permanent wilting point' and may die of drought even though in fact the compost contains plenty of moisture locked up in its too-tight pores; and matters will be made worse in such conditions by oxygen starvation, often combined with a build-up of poisonous concentrations of chemicals.

Another practice that is called into question is the old custom of putting 'crocks' (broken pieces of clay pot) over the hole at the bottom of a pot before putting in the compost, 'to improve drainage'. After careful investigation at the Institute it was found that because of the effect that the lower layers in soil have on draining the upper part, the compost in shallow pots will remain wetter after watering than compost in tall pots. Since crocking reduces the depth of compost, it too will make the compost above the crocks wetter. It seems, therefore, that the tedious process of crocking, which must have taken countless hours of potting time over the years, is quite unnecessary, at any rate with modern composts – which is just as well, since in these days of plastic pots bits of broken clay pot are not so plentiful.

When the young plants in their seed compost have grown big enough to be transferred to larger quarters – that is, when the roots have reached the wall of the pot, but before they have become pot-bound – they can be 'potted on' into the stronger and more nourishing potting compost. Take a 3-inch (7.5 cm) or

3½-inch (9 cm) pot, put a layer of potting compost in the bottom, knock the plant out of its pot, place it, with its ball of seed compost filled with roots intact, on that bottom layer in the new pot and fill up the space around it with more potting compost. Tap the bottom of the pot smartly on the bench or other surface, water well and allow to drain. If the new compost has sunk below the level of the surface of the original compost round the plant, top up with more to make the surface level. Resist the impulse to press down the added compost.

As plants become bigger they need more food, both to sustain their increased growth and to replace the amount they have used. To cater for their greater appetite, there are two further variants of the John Innes potting compost which contain increased amounts of nourishment. The ordinary version, for which the recipe has been given on page 78 and on to which young plants are weaned from their seed compost, is known as JIP1, and the two more nourishing variants are known as JIP2 and JIP3. The three versions all contain exactly the same quantities of loam, peat and sand, but JIP2 has twice the amount, and JIP3 three times the amount, of JI Base and chalk. On the whole it is generally considered that there is sufficient nourishment in JIP1 for a plant in a 3½-inch (9 cm) pot. When it outgrows that it will benefit from being put into JIP2 when potted on into a 4½ inch (11 cm) or 5 inch (12.5 cm) size, and the same should be adequate up to 7 inches (17.5 cm). After that, if you want to grow any plants into large specimens, occupying pots of 8-inch (20 cm) diameter or more, they can manage the full JIP3 formula.

Later in a plant's life, when the fertilizer in the compost is getting used up, it will be necessary to start giving supplementary feeds. A formula for a suitable liquid feed was worked out at the John Innes Institution, consisting of 15 parts by weight of ammonium sulphate, 2.75 parts of potassium nitrate and 2.25 parts of mono-ammonium phosphate. The recommended dilution, worked out after many experiments, was ½ oz (15g) to 1 gallon (4.5 litres) of water, to be given, for general purposes and to pot-bound plants during the growing season, about once a week. The feed should be used within twenty-four hours of mixing, otherwise some of the phosphate will be precipitated out of solution and wasted. Because of this, many people nowadays prefer to use one of the many brands of liquid fertilizer sold in bottles at all garden shops. As a general rule it is best to use a high-nitrogen product during the first half of the season, when growth is at its most vigorous, and a low-nitrogen one later in the year, when days are shortening and growth slackening. During the winter, supplementary feeding is needed very infrequently, if at all; a plant that is resting rather than growing is incapable of taking in much food. More and more people nowadays are turning from liquid feeds to the newer slow-release fertilizers in granular form, whose advantages are described on page 151.

Soil-less composts

Though large quantities of John Innes composts are still made and used by both amateur and professional growers, during the past few years there has been a considerable development of new types of compost containing no soil at all but consisting of peat to which has been added a quantity of sand, grit, perlite or similar material to keep the texture open and porous, plus precisely measured amounts of chemicals to provide nourishment and to bring the compost to the correct balance between acidity and alkalinity. These 'soil-less' composts were developed largely because good loam had become somewhat scarce and so a substitute had to be found, but they have proved to have certain very real advantages. They are light and easy to handle, they are practically unvarying in quality, and the ingredients do not need to be sterilized, because they do not favour the growth of harmful organisms which are only too ready to infect soil.

They are also ideally suited to the modern plastic pot, which with its non-porous walls prevents them from losing moisture too rapidly (the one possible snag with soil-less composts is that if they are allowed to become too dry they are extremely difficult to moisten again). It should be remembered that the John Innes composts were developed in the days of the old clay pots, which lost water much more rapidly by evaporation through the sides; indeed, many successful growers, when using John Innes composts in plastic pots, add a little extra sand or grit to the mixture to offset the water-retaining properties of the plastic.

Do not attempt to mix your own soil-less composts: to do so successfully needs proper equipment for accurate mixing, measuring, weighing, testing and monitoring performance. In any case, even if you possessed the necessary equipment and knowledge it is doubtful if you could produce this type of compost any more cheaply than the fairly modest cost of buying one of the many brands you will find to choose from at your local supplier.

Note that the vast majority of plants will grow very well in the standard John Innes and soil-less composts. There are, however, a few lime-haters, such as certain rhododendrons and heathers, which will not grow well except in mixtures that do not contain lime. For them there are special lime-free composts available – or if you want to grow them in John Innes composts of your own mixing you can do so by omitting the chalk from the mixture.

HYGIENE

Having dealt with potting methods and with composts, let us now return to the question of scrupulous cleanliness mentioned at the beginning of this chapter. In the old days, when obsession with cleanliness was at its height, there was one glaring source of infection which went unchecked, and which must have made all the elaborate precautions in the interests of hygiene more or less useless. That source of infection was the potting soil itself. Though the hours of hard work spent scrubbing out pots till every trace of dirt had gone may have been good for the souls of those who did the scrubbing, we can now see from our superior vantage point in time that the whole thing was pretty meaningless while the soil that went into the pots remained unsterilized. Small wonder that results were unpredictable and mortality high.

Now that we have sterilized composts at our disposal, however, all those habits of cleanliness and attention to hygiene make perfectly good sense. It would be the height of folly to allow that sterilized compost to become infected by disease organisms or pests through failure to take routine precautions. All pots and other containers should be clean outside and inside before they are used or stored. Benches and staging should be scrubbed whenever they show signs of getting grubby. Unsterilized soil should never be allowed to come into contact with – or even near – sterilized soil or compost. Fallen leaves, and dead or dying plants, should be taken away and disposed of before they can spread infection. Rubbish, if allowed to accumulate, forms a perfect breeding place for pests and diseases, so it must be removed immediately.

CHAPTER SIX

Transplanting

EVERYTHING THAT HAS BEEN LEARNED about the needs of young plants shows that they can be ruined, maybe for life, by being uprooted from the surroundings they have become used to and put into an alien environment. Plants, like children, need stability; they cannot simply be shifted around at the whim of their owners.

The first thing, then, is never to transplant at all unless absolutely necessary – particularly with plants that have a short life cycle. Even with the gentlest and most careful handling there may simply not be time for an annual, with only six months or so to live, to form completely new attachments. It may put on a brave show, but is unlikely to do as well as if it had been allowed to finish its days in the place where it first put down roots.

And that is true not only of plants in the flower garden, but even of those vegetables that are traditionally transplanted. Recent research has shown, for instance, that cauliflowers sown direct into their final quarters can give greatly superior crops to those raised in a seed-bed and planted out later (see p. 56). Even some tender or half-hardy kinds which are commonly started into growth in pots under glass and planted out when the danger of frost is past have been shown to do better if sown in the open in their final positions. Sweet corn, even sown when one or two frosts can still be expected, will usually overtake pot-grown plants put out when the danger is over and grow to be much sturdier, without the need for support that transplanting so often entails.

Some people get the best of both worlds by sowing under cloches, so avoiding the upset of transplanting while still giving some protection in the early stages. Do not remove the cloches till the seedlings are a few inches high, by which time the frosts should be over. But some say that even this small amount of molly-coddling is a mistake: though taller and apparently more advanced at first, the plants will be more easily blown over and so more in need of support than the more self-reliant plants raised without any protection at all.

TRANSPLANTING HALF-HARDY ANNUALS

There are many plants grown in our gardens that came originally from tropical or sub-tropical climates. Though the efforts of plant-breeders may have made them much more tolerant of cool conditions, they do not have a long enough growing season to reach maturity during our short summers. These tender plants include many of the attractive and colourful half-hardy annuals grown for their flowers as well as others – such as tomatoes, sweet peppers and aubergines – grown for their fruit. At present all these have to be raised in heat during the miserably short days of late winter or early spring, and grown on in protected conditions, if they are to be sufficiently developed by planting out time to reach maturity in their new quarters before the shortening days of autumn and the onset of frosts put an end to their lives. (Even here, though, plant-breeders are working hard to produce 'infant prodigies', which develop so fast that they can be sown outdoors in the summer and still have time to reach full maturity in the few months that remain before they are killed by the cold. They would then be able to spend the whole of their short lives in the same place and never experience the shock of transplanting. One or two of these early developers are already available to amateurs, such as the tomato 'Pixie', and more will certainly follow.)

Pricking out

Half-hardy annuals are still most often raised in shallow boxes or trays. Usually they are sown in seed compost in one such container and then transferred to another by an operation known as 'pricking out': as soon as they have produced two or three leaves they are gently lifted from the compost, using a small fork or a special instrument of similar design (a process made easier if there is a fair amount of vermiculite and/or sand in the compost, so that the tiny, delicate roots come out easily without breaking), and planted out 2 inches (5 cm) or so apart in the new tray. The compost in the new tray should be moist, but not soggy. Planting holes may be made in it with a pencil, a pointed stick or a finger (mini-dibbers made of plastic, or even of stainless steel, may be bought for the purpose, but they are quite unnecessary). The seedlings to be transferred should be lifted by a leaf – *not* by the stem, for fear of its being pinched – and lowered carefully into the holes; tiny ones such as begonias, with leaves so small that they are difficult to get hold of, can be held with a forked twig or with a plant label with a small V-shaped notch cut in the end.

Great care must be taken to see that each seedling goes right down into the hole and does not get caught against the side, otherwise it may be hung in an air pocket, and the root may shrivel; besides, the base of the stem may get kinked and broken when the hole is filled in. It is not always easy to avoid this, especially if little or no compost is left clinging to the root to give it weight. Even the steadiest hand may wobble, or a slight air movement may occur. As a result the tip of the root touches the side of the hole and stubbornly clings there instead of going down inside; you pull the seedling out and try again, but the same thing happens. An easy way to deal with this is to dip the tip of the root into water (lukewarm, not ice-cold, or it may get a nasty shock) and then touch some dry sand with it; a few particles of the sand will stick to the root tip and weigh it down. It will then obediently allow itself to be lowered into the hole to its full length.

As each seedling is pricked out, the compost should be well firmed around it, so that the root is in intimate contact with the compost throughout its length. To achieve this, it is a good idea to do what the professionals do: after planting, push the dibber, stick or finger down into the compost to one side of the seedling and about half an inch (1 cm) from it, and then press inwards towards the seedling; this will firm the compost against it. After the pricking out has been completed, water gently, using a fine rose, to settle the compost round the roots.

It is important that the pricking out should be done as soon as the seedlings are large enough to handle; if left till they become overcrowded, they will be pallid and drawn, and much more susceptible to disease – particularly the fungal attack known as 'damping off', which can cause a whole trayful of young plants to collapse and fall down dead within a few hours.

If carried out early enough, pricking out is a form of transplanting unlikely to lead to complications: the young root is a simple affair and has not had time to form many attachments, except perhaps to particles of compost with which it is in close contact and which in any case will be moved with it, so that it does not suffer any wrench. If all goes well the pricked-out seedlings should continue to grow as if nothing had happened, and by the time the weather is warm enough for them to be planted out they should have become sturdy plants robust enough to face the next, and more traumatic, operation.

Transplanting into the garden

Unfortunately when it comes to taking ordinary box-grown seedlings out of their container in order to transplant them there is no way of preventing some of the roots being torn off and left behind. If you have raised them yourself you can take your time over the operation and exercise great care, but however gentle you are you cannot help damaging a large proportion of the tiny, vulnerable hair-roots, which are almost invisible to the naked eye and on which the plants depend to take in nourishment. If, on the other hand, you buy them from a nursery or garden centre, or worse still from a barrow or market stall, the busy seller will have no time for gentle handling but will tend to rip out the plants as quickly as possible and you will be lucky if a quarter of the roots remain undamaged. For this reason many plants are now sold in what are called 'strips', which are channels of plastic filled with compost in which the seedlings are spaced 2 inches (5 cm) or so apart. You have to pay a little more for plants grown in this way, but it is well worth it; the roots will not remain totally undamaged when you separate the seedlings to plant them out, but they will suffer much less than those grown in boxes.

The same is true of seedlings grown in pots. As explained in the chapter on potting, roots are much less likely to cling to the sides of plastic containers than to the old-fashioned clay pots; and if a good watering is given an hour or two beforehand to provide lubrication there should be no wrenching or tearing. All the same, even with plastic, some attachments will almost certainly have been formed between the minute hair-roots and the container – and even the breaking of these tiny attachments is bound to affect the seedling's progress to some extent.

That is one of the reasons for the increasing popularity of soil blocks. Though these may originally have been developed as an economy measure, because of the increasing costs of pots and other containers, they have proved their superiority in many ways – so much so that a large number of commercial growers nowadays have abandoned all other methods of raising seedlings. Each block is a separate, self-supporting cube, measuring 1½ inches (4 cm) each way, and made of compost just cohesive enough to hold together when moulded. Soil-based seed compost will do at a pinch, but it is much better to use specially made peat blocking compost, which contains an adhesive material to prevent the blocks from falling to pieces, and a wetting agent to make sure of uniform moisture throughout. Professionals use machines that produce several blocks in one operation, but amateurs can buy a small gadget that makes one block at a time, with a small depression in the top in which the seeds are sown.

The blocks are extruded from the mould into an ordinary seed-tray, so that they stand side by side – nearly touching but not quite. Seeds can be sown singly, one to each block, but it is usually better to sow two or three to allow for failures and thin the resulting seedlings to one. Do this by snipping off the doomed seedlings with a pair of scissors, so that the roots of the remaining one are not disturbed.

Each seedling grows fast and well in its own block, with no competition from other plants to contend with, and develops a splendid root system, which fills the block but stops short of breaking through to the outside – the fine roots have a built-in mechanism which prevents them from making their way into the air, where they might shrivel and die. Each seedling can then be planted out without injury, and into soil that might be too wet or too dry for exposed roots.

Unfortunately soil blocks are not quite robust enough to be subjected to the rough and tumble of normal methods of transport, so they are not yet usually available through ordinary marketing outlets. But you could raise block-grown seedlings yourself, or look for one of the few garden centres that are beginning to sell them – but be careful on the drive home not to jolt them too much, or they might fall to pieces. It would be safer to buy plants in peat or paper pulp pots. These are treated so as to keep them intact till they are planted out, when the moisture in the surrounding soil causes them to soften so that the roots can push their way through into the earth. So long as the ground is damp enough (but not soggy), there is little or no check to plants set out in pots of this type. But, of course, they cost a bit more.

TRANSPLANTING HARDY PLANTS

By methods such as these half-hardy and tender plants can be made to flower earlier and more abundantly, and to produce stronger and more vigorous growth. With hardier subjects, as has already been pointed out, the ideal is not to transplant at all but to leave them to grow to maturity in their original home. However, there are circumstances when it is best to forget about the ideal and to settle for transplanting even hardy things. It may be that there is not enough space to sow them direct into their final quarters, because the ground is occupied by other things, which will not be cleared away till the season is well advanced; that is the chief reason why Brussels sprouts and other members of the cabbage family are usually sown in a seed-bed and planted out later. (Though you are still likely to get much better results if the seedlings are raised in pots or soil-blocks.)

Another good reason for transplanting is that the ground can be cleared of weeds; the cultivated plants can then take over the ground, and any new weed seedlings will be at a competitive disadvantage. If sown direct, it is the cultivated plants that are likely to be at a disadvantage, unless you have the time, energy and patience to remove weeds as they germinate and before they take over. Some commercial growers of field crops nowadays reckon that the setback caused to the plants by moving them is more than compensated for by being able to clear the ground completely before transplanting takes place.

Where trees and shrubs are concerned, it is normal practice to transplant them. There are several good reasons: first, people usually like to plant something of a fair size, so that it is already worth looking at when it is put in. Second, even plants that are perfectly hardy when they have reached a fair size may need a certain amount of protection in the early years of life. Third, most of the choicest varieties have to be propagated by vegetative methods. This requires skill – and sometimes techniques and equipment possessed only by specialists; it also takes time before the new plants are independent enough to lead a separate existence.

WHEN TO TRANSPLANT?

Where transplanting has to be done, it should be carried out as soon as possible after it is safe to do so. Experiments at the National Vegetable Research Station have shown that nearly all vegetables can be transplanted at the early seedling stage with little or no check to growth. The older the plant, however, the greater is the transplanting check. The check is most severe in vegetables that are flowering, because roots are not produced so readily at this stage of growth. Experiments with tomatoes showed that those transplanted when in flower gave an average yield 20 per cent lower than those transplanted before the flowering stage.

As explained in chapter 7, the onset of flowering is accompanied by profound changes. To quote Peter J. Salter, of the National Vegetable Research Station, in that highly informative book *Know and Grow Vegetables*: 'In general, whenever annual plants pass through the flowering and fruiting phases of development root growth is very much reduced because the plant gives priority to the development of flowers, fruit and seeds.' Because of this reduced activity, roots do not grow vigorously into the surrounding soil, exploring it for water. Consequently they become reliant on rain, or failing that on artificial watering. This is known as the 'moisture-sensitive' stage: the plants demand constant drinks of water, and if they are denied it even for quite a short time they are likely to droop. So plants transplanted when already in flower may have to be propped up – unlike plants with a wider and deeper root system, which can usually stand up by themselves.

What goes for vegetables also goes for other plants. Though it is obviously most important for annuals to build up a good root system quickly, because they have only a brief life in which to grow and flower, longer-lived plants – herbaceous perennials, shrubs and trees – should also be put into their permanent quarters while they are young and adaptable. The older they get the less able they are to put down roots and settle into new surroundings.

That is why it is best to ignore attempts by nurserymen to

persuade you to have an 'instant garden' by buying trees and shrubs several years old, and big enough to have what they call a 'mature look'. You will not only save yourself money by buying something smaller and younger, but within a year or two the younger plant will almost certainly outstrip the older one, both in size and in self-reliance.

What is the best time of year for transplanting? Obviously tender and half-hardy plants cannot be put into the open ground till the frosts – or at any rate the hard frosts – are over (though with some protection from cold nights by means of cloches, polythene tunnels, or even an inverted jam-jar or two, some of the almost hardy subjects can be planted out a week or two earlier). It is worse than useless to try to beat the season by planting them out too soon. Tomatoes put into cold soil will repay your cruelty by refusing to grow: their roots may well rot, and if they survive they will most likely be permanently crippled, their yield sub-standard in quality and quantity.

Hardy plants have traditionally been planted out between late autumn and early spring. Herbaceous perennials are usually transplanted when the tops have died down and deciduous trees and shrubs when they have lost their leaves. Evergreens, on the other hand, have been found to do better if the operation is performed either in mid-autumn or in mid-spring. This is because the leaves give off water, which has to be supplied by the roots; it is important, therefore, that new roots should be encouraged to grow out into the soil as quickly as possible, and this will only happen if the soil is warm enough. Naturally, it is with plants dug up from the ground that the time of transplanting is most critical, since large parts of the roots are bound to have been torn off and left behind in the course of lifting, particularly if thick woody roots had formed. These are not only the most difficult to heal, but also the least capable of producing new growth.

In the old days, when labour was cheap, nurserymen used to have their trees and shrubs regularly dug up and replanted, so that a mass of thinner fibrous roots developed instead of thick woody taproots. Nowdays such methods have become almost prohibitively expensive, since labour is the costliest part of production. Besides, during the last few years more and more plants have been bought from garden centres, many of which propagate little or nothing themselves, but simply sell plants produced by specialists.

THE CONTAINER REVOLUTION

Since the efficient handling and selling of the plants is what makes a garden centre profitable, packaging for the greatest convenience of buyer and seller, as well as for keeping the merchandise in good condition and making it as attractive-looking as possible, is as important as the plants themselves. That is why trees and shrubs, which not many years ago would have had to be dug from the open ground, are now commonly grown and sold in containers. One of the things that have made this possible is the development of black polythene, which can be made up into containers of various sizes. These are now used by the million to raise and market young stock, and have some obvious advantages.

First, they are easy to transport without breaking. Second, they enable the young plant to be put into the ground with its ball of soil intact and with the minimum of root disturbance. Third, as is stressed by gardening journalists and by publicity put out by the trade, container-grown trees and shrubs can be planted out at any time of the year, not just in the cold and miserable months. While there is some truth in this last claim, transplanting, even of container-grown subjects, is still best done in the autumn or spring: it is tempting fate to plant things out in the summer, when the soil may be too hot and dry to invite new roots to invade it and when watering may even be restricted or forbidden.

A new danger

Recent research has shown that, in spite of all their advantages, container-grown plants may face certain dangers from which plants grown in the open ground are protected by nature. During the severe winter of 1978–9, many plants that would have survived a normal winter died, but it was noticed that the casualty rate was much higher among plants in containers than among those of the same kind growing in the earth. In looking for the cause, scientists at Cornell University in the USA found that, among other things, the stems of many shrubs can stand much more intense cold than the roots; in some cases the parts above the ground can happily put up with temperatures nearly 30°F (17°C) lower than the point at which the parts beneath the surface would be killed. The reason seems to be that in hardy species the

93

stems are able to concentrate in their sap sugars and other chemicals which, like anti-freeze in a car, prevent ice from forming. Roots do not have this ability, so they remain vulnerable to icing.

This difference in hardiness between roots and shoots has no doubt developed because in natural conditions the underground parts are much better protected against the cold. In the open, soil provides an excellent blanket, since even in the coldest weather frost rarely penetrates much below the surface layer. The soil in a container, however, can easily be frozen solid by a single hard frost. To make matters worse, young roots are more susceptible to cold than older ones, and it is these young roots that are mostly found towards the outside of the soil in the container, where freezing is at its most severe.

The result of all this can be that an apparently strong and healthy container-grown plant, transplanted lovingly into somebody's garden, starts encouragingly into growth as the days get warmer and longer, but quickly begins to wither because the roots have been frozen to death.

One way in which many plant dealers attempt to reduce the risk is by plunging the containers in gravel, sand, peat or some such material to protect them from the cold. The possible snag is that young roots may penetrate the drainage holes that containers must have to prevent their contents from becoming waterlogged; having escaped, the roots will then branch out and explore the outside world of gravel or whatever, so that when the plant is lifted it suffers some of the very root damage that growing it in a container was supposed to avoid. Some nurserymen and plant dealers have developed methods of overcoming, or at least reducing, the problem by interposing plastic film between the container and the surrounding material; this may not prevent the more adventurous roots from making their way through the drainage holes, but it does at any rate stop them from forming attachments from which they will later have to be torn.

Many nurserymen now protect their container-grown plants by overwintering them in tunnel-shaped structures covered with transparent polythene, and this does cut down very considerably the number of casualties from freezing. It can cause problems, however. On sunny days high temperatures can build up in the tunnel, even though it is quite cold outside, and this may prevent the plants from becoming fully dormant, or even start them into premature growth.

Trees and shrubs raised in the old-fashioned way in an open-ground nursery, and dug up for transplanting, were not subjected to this particular danger, whatever other defects that method may have had. Still, the advantages of raising young stock in containers easily outweigh the disadvantages. The container revolution is bound to continue, and as it continues no doubt means will be developed to overcome the problems posed by hardy plants with not-so-hardy roots.

Meanwhile, the most sensible thing for the gardener to do is to transplant in the autumn, while there is still some warmth in the ground, so that new roots can be encouraged to make their way into the soil before winter cold puts a stop to their growth. This has the added advantage that you can choose the best-looking plants before they are sold to somebody else.

If that is impossible, it might be best to wait till the container-grown plants in the nursery have produced plenty of new growth in the spring, so that you can be sure that the ones you choose have survived the winter with an undamaged root system. In this case you will have to see to it that the plant is not allowed to fail for lack of water. With autumn planting the things to fear are wet and cold; with spring planting the hazards are dryness and heat.

DEALING WITH HOMESICKNESS

All transplanting involves taking a young growing thing from familiar into unfamiliar surroundings. The important point, if the operation is to be successful, is to make sure that the new environment should be as welcoming as the old one.

Unfortunately all too many people just shove the new plant unceremoniously into the ground. Maybe they stamp the ground round it, because they have some idea that that is the right thing to do, and then give it a bucketful of water, which stands in a puddle on the trampled surface doing more harm than good. But they do not pause to consider that so far it has enjoyed a certain standard of living. If it has been properly raised, the mixture in which it has grown has been rather special, providing the roots with something to cling to, and the right amount of moisture, air and food.

In chapter 3 advice is given on the necessary groundwork to provide plants with the ingredients for a good life. At the time of transplanting – probably the most difficult period of adjustment that a young plant can undergo – extra effort to ease the process will be amply repaid. Just as everything possible should be done to help a newly uprooted child to form fresh relationships, so a newly transplanted tree or shrub should be encouraged to put out roots into its new surroundings as soon as possible.

Before the plant is taken out of its container the planting hole should be dug, somewhat wider than the diameter of the container. The bottom of the hole should be loosened with a fork, and plenty of peat, compost or well-rotted manure mixed into it. The bottom should then be made firm by lightly treading it down, but *not* by stamping hard. To make sure that the plant is put into the ground at the same depth as it was previously (planting too deep is a common fault), lay a stick across the hole to show where the surface of the soil will come when it has been filled in; then place the plant so that the surface of its compost, if it is container-grown, or the mark left by the soil, if it has been dug from the open ground, comes level with the stick.

If a stake is needed to prevent a young tree from being rocked by the wind, or even blown over, before it has had time to put out enough new roots to anchor itself firmly, drive in the stake before you begin planting, so as to avoid the root damage that is almost certain to occur if it is put in afterwards. If the soil seems dry, give the hole a thorough watering, and then wait till the water has completely drained away before going any further.

Do not remove plants from their containers – or in the case of plants grown in the open ground do not unwrap the roots – until just before planting them out. If you are going to plant out several, deal with them one at a time; it is surprising how quickly the vital hair-roots can shrivel when exposed to the air. For the same reason, a cool day with an overcast sky should be chosen for transplanting if possible; a certain amount of mist, or even a light drizzle (but not heavy rain), will provide just the right conditions to ensure that the roots do not dry out during the operation. It goes without saying that no attempt should be made to transplant when the ground is frozen, or for that matter when the weather forecast threatens frost. In such conditions the best thing to do is to put the plants, still in their containers and/or wrappers, in a cool but frost-free shed or garage (but not in a greenhouse, which may be too warm) till things are more comfortable.

Having placed the plant at the correct height in the hole, fill in the soil a portion at a time, incorporating peat, compost, well-rotted manure or similar material as you go (if the ground is heavy, some sharp sand or grit will help too). This makes an inviting mixture for young roots to invade. A dusting of bonemeal as work proceeds will help to stimulate root growth.

With container-grown plants, tread each portion firmly before adding the next, but do not stamp it down hard or you will make it difficult for the roots to penetrate. Traditional bare-root trees and shrubs will have been brought up in fairly spartan conditions and such earth as remains clinging to their roots when they are dug up will probably be not unlike ordinary garden soil. Besides, since much of the root system will have become naked during lifting and transporting the most important thing is to get it into close contact with the earth as quickly as possible, and this is usually best done in the old way, by a combination of vigorous shaking of the plant during transplanting – so as to shake soil down between the roots – and equally vigorous trampling.

This, however, is not appropriate for modern container-grown plants. The roots are not naked but completely clothed, and the growing medium in which they have been reared has accustomed them if not to soft living at least to a certain style. They are not therefore likely to venture readily into hard, unfamiliar ground, but may take the easy way of turning inwards on themselves and continuing to go round in circles in the comfortable compost with which they are familiar, till at last they can find no more space to grow. The plant will wilt, turn sickly in appearance, and probably die. When you pull it up to see what went wrong, you will find the roots clinging together in a tight ball, thin and brown instead of plump and white-tipped, and very likely rotting because they have been standing in water which has been unable to drain away through the impervious earth – or, at the other extreme, dry and withered because no water has been able to reach them from the surrounding soil.

It would not perhaps be too fanciful to say in such circumstances that the plant's death had resulted from its withdrawal from outside contact because of homesickness brought about through ignorant and insensitive transplanting.

CHAPTER SEVEN

Adolescence and its problems

As with human offspring, profound changes take place in the young plant as it emerges from childhood and prepares to take its place among adults. Some plants show less marked changes than others, but nearly all go through a period of development designed to fit them for their sexual role.

THE ONSET OF PUBERTY

The changes that come about in plants are, like those in human and other animals, produced largely by the action of hormones, those chemical substances that regulate growth and development. The most obvious changes are in the rate of growth. The exuberant and rapid growth during infancy and early development tends to slow down for a while just before puberty, as the hormonal balance alters. Depending on the nature of the plant, this pause may last for a shorter or longer time, from maybe only an hour or two in the case of an annual to weeks, months or even years in the case of a tree or shrub. There is nothing to worry about in this slowing down of growth, so long as in other respects the plant seems to be healthy. It is a natural stage on the road to adulthood.

At the end of this pause there is often a sudden surge of growth, when the plant shoots up so fast that you can almost watch it grow. It is like the stage at which boys and girls suddenly start to grow out of all their clothes, and to develop enormous appetites because of the extra demands made by this speeded up growth. Sheer quantity, rather than the actual kind of food, is what seems to matter at this hungry point of development; and there is some experimental evidence that much the same sort of thing goes for plants too. Choosiness comes later.

The age of puberty

There are at least a quarter of a million different species of flowering plants alone; add to that figure more than half as many non-flowering kinds, and the total number of species comes to about 400,000. They range from tiny organisms, visible only under a microscope, to huge trees which have taken more than 2,000 years to grow, and are not only the biggest but the oldest living things on earth.

With such an enormous number of different sorts of plants it is not surprising that the age at which they reach puberty varies from a few weeks to a hundred years or so. Obviously annuals must get through their entire life cycle within a year if the species is to continue. If from that year is subtracted not only the winter, when no growth takes place, but also the time the flower takes to develop and become sexually mature enough for fertilization, and then the time the fruit takes to ripen and mature its seeds, it will be seen that at most only a few weeks of infancy are left between 'birth' (i.e. germination) and puberty.

Some plants, particularly those from places with cold, harsh winters and scorching summers, may have to cram their whole life into a very short period between the time when the ground thaws sufficiently for germination to take place and the time when it becomes so parched that plants growing in it shrivel and die. Such short-lived plants are called ephemerals, as are those that also have brief lives but enjoy a kinder climate, so that they may produce two, or three, or even more generations in the course of a single season. Even they, however, have a short period of infancy during which they are markedly different in appearance and behaviour from the adults they will so soon become.

INFANTILE DEVELOPMENT

When a seed sprouts, the embryo inside breaks through the skin and starts a transformation that will end in its becoming a plant. It cannot yet be properly called a plant, because it is not fully formed: indeed, the embryos of many species are so rudimentary at this stage that they have few if any of the features by which we recognize a plant. That is a fundamental difference between the reproduction of plants and of people: in humans the development from embryo to foetus goes on inside the mother's womb, so that by the time the baby is born it is fully formed, but plants go through most of their development after they have emerged as seeds from what botanists call the ovary. So to use the word birth for the germination of a seed, as is often done, is hardly appropriate.

Most seeds contain a store of food to provide the emerging seedling with something to live on till it is able to take nourishment from its surroundings. There are exceptions, notably orchids, whose seeds have no food store and so cannot survive in their natural surroundings unless they are given the energy for growth from sugar provided by a certain type of fungus. Millions of orchids are raised in special laboratories, on sterilized jelly containing sugar, chemicals and vitamins.

In most kinds of seed the food is stored in what are commonly called seed-leaves, known to botanists as cotyledon. These are often the first parts of the seedling to appear above the soil, where they spread themselves out and turn green, taking on the appearance of leaves. At the same time, unseen, the first root is pushing its way downwards, pulled by the force of gravity and pushed by an urge to get away from the light. Next, branches appear, producing a network of rootlets, from which grow the hairs through which water and dissolved salts are sucked in. After the seed-leaves the true leaves develop, together with the shoot which carries them. These are often very different from the seed-leaves; instead of remaining simple in outline they may develop saw-toothed edges, or lobes, like the fingers of a hand; the next may grow into compound leaves, with two or three separate leaflets, and the next may have five, or seven or more leaflets, like those of a rose; further leaves may have a dozen or more leaflets in pairs along a stalk, like an ash tree, or develop in an even more complicated manner.

After the first few leaves have unfolded, the leaves may become bigger as the plant increases in size, but they look the same. But underneath this apparent sameness potent chemical substances are building up in the sap-stream, like the hormones that accumulate in our own bloodstreams before puberty.

ARRESTED DEVELOPMENT

Some plants, like some people, never grow up. They remain in a state of permanent childhood. In most human societies nowadays arrested development among children is caused by some inbuilt fault of the genetic structure; it is rarely deliberately brought about by the actions of parents or others in authority. As recently as the last century, however, devout fathers would have a son castrated in early childhood, so as to retain the piping infant voice that would enable the *castrato*, as he was called, to continue to sing treble in the choir all his life.

With some garden plants, very deliberate methods are used to keep them in a permanent state of arrested development. The methods involve some pretty drastic cutting, which preserves the juvenile characteristics that those who grow them find so attractive. Such cherished permanent juveniles can, of course, only be grown for their foliage, not their flowers, because flowers are the very sexual organs that such plants are being prevented from developing. They are really garden pets, like neutered cats, never any trouble, always tidy to have about the place, but incapable of sexual reproduction (though the plants, unlike the doctored cats, can be propagated, appropriately enough, by cuttings).

An example of such forcibly imposed permanent childhood to be seen in many gardens is a beech hedge, which is allowed to grow to a certain height and then kept constantly clipped to prevent any attempt to grow into a tree. The gardener who attends conscientiously to the clipping is rewarded by the beautiful russet-coloured juvenile foliage, which clings on throughout the winter – unlike the adult leaves of a beech tree, which drop off when autumn comes. Other hedging plants, kept closely trimmed and never allowed to produce any flowering shoots, can be kept indefinitely in an immature stage, with nothing ever appearing but the juvenile type of foliage. The same is true of those specimens of yew or box clipped into the shape of animals and birds which are still to be found in a few old-fashioned gardens.

Permanent infancy

Though continual clipping may have preserved a childish condition, the sexual urge is still strong. If the clipping is stopped for more than a short period, puberty may still assert itself even at quite an advanced age: a new type of shoot may appear, of more mature character, and intent on sexual development. Then it may be too late to restore the plant completely to its juvenile state, for it may need such severe cutting back as to amount to major surgery, which can give such a shock to the plant's system that it dies.

There are, by contrast, some garden plants that seem to have lost the sexual urge entirely. They remain in a permanent state of infancy, never show any signs of puberty, and need no cutting or restraint to stop them from developing into adults. Some of these permanent juveniles are highly esteemed as garden plants, especially where space is limited, because they are models of self-control, neat and restrained in habit, keeping themselves to themselves, and rarely if ever needing to be cut. Several of the best are to be found among the dwarf cypresses and their related conifers. They are slow-growing and compact, with densely arranged juvenile foliage, and it is almost unheard of for any wayward shoot to venture beyond the precise regularity of the plant's outline.

A dainty example of these conifers that never grow up is *Chamaecyparis pisifera* 'Boulevard', a small bush of such exact conical shape that it looks as if it might have been turned on a lathe. The soft, feathery foliage is pale steel-blue during the summer, turning purple in the winter. It was found in the USA in the 1930s as a 'sport' (a mutant branch) of the variety 'Squarrosa', which though a more robust grower is itself also a perpetual juvenile.

Identity problems

Because botanists recognize plants mainly by their sexual characteristics, they were for a long time baffled by these perpetual juveniles. Since no sexual development ever took place, and there was therefore nothing to identify them by, what were they and what should they be called?

Because many of these varieties were discovered in the middle of the last century, when we did not know as much about the subject of juvenility as we do now, they were mistakenly thought to be something completely new and different, and reproductively mysterious. Botanists, always glad to immortalize themselves by inventing new names, did so enthusiastically when faced with these strange discoveries. Of the names they coined for the supposedly new type of plant, most have disappeared, but one, *Retinospora*, still sometimes appears in the lists of a few very old-fashioned plant dealers. It is applied to several of the juvenile forms of *Chamaecyparis*, such as *C. pisifera* 'Boulevard' and the remarkable slow-growing dwarf *C. obtusa* 'Sanderi', still sometimes called *Retinospora sanderi*, and highly desirable as a self-disciplined subject in a sheltered spot. Some nurserymen mistakenly call it 'Ericoides'.

The Japanese cedar is normally fully equipped with rather obvious organs of both sexes on the same tree, the male ones a striking orange-red and the female ones maturing as globular cones in the first year. Its botanical name is *Cryptomeria japonica*. A variety of it with soft, feathery juvenile foliage was discovered in Japan by the famous plant-collector Thomas Lobb, who introduced it to Britain in 1854. Its graceful charm and its extremely neat habit of growth brought it instant popularity among gardeners, and eight years after its introduction it was awarded the Royal Horticultural Society's highest award, the First Class Certificate. Since then it has been propagated continuously from cuttings. It is grown in thousands upon thousands of gardens, and is sold by nearly every nurseryman and garden centre. Yet during the century and a quarter that has gone by since its introduction it has never grown up: it bears the same feathery juvenile foliage.

But the story goes back far beyond Lobb's happy find. Nobody knows how long *Cryptomeria japonica* 'Elegans', as it is now called, had been grown in Japan before then, but it may have been for centuries. As we know, the Japanese have a particular liking for small plants of a formal kind; that is why they have perfected the art of dwarfing trees and shrubs, known as Bonsai. No doubt at some time in the past a Japanese gardener with an eye for such things noticed a specially desirable shoot on a Japanese cedar with more compact growth and foliage that stayed feathery and soft after the other shoots had started to show signs of adulthood. He took a cutting of the special shoot, rooted it and found that it kept its juvenile state as it grew. Generations of Japanese gardeners continued to take cuttings, each time choosing the most compact and attractive shoot, till finally the form was selected that is now known as 'Elegans'. (The process did not stop there: in the 1880s an even more compact form, with leaves that turn a rich purple in winter, appeared as a sport from 'Elegans' and was called 'Elegans Compacta', by which name it is still known.)

Can permanent juveniles be produced at will?

Some professionals are attempting to multiply the number of such sports by physical and chemical means, so as to have more to choose from, but the amateur must still rely on a keen eye for the chance natural occurrences of sports. They do not occur very often, and the number of species in which fixed juvenility can be found is limited, but if a sport should turn up in your garden that appeals to you it is worth trying to propagate it from cuttings. If it is left on the plant where it appears it may soon die, not being able to compete with the more vigorous shoots around it; but if it can be got on to its own roots it may thrive. What is more, it may be of commercial value; many famous and well-loved varieties have arisen in the gardens of amateurs with a talent for spotting the unusual.

Look for such juvenile sports at the base of the plant; the higher up a shoot appears, the less likely it is to show infantile characteristics.

STIRRINGS OF ADOLESCENCE

The vast majority of garden plants will come through the infantile stage and undergo the sometimes dramatic changes necessary to fit them for their sexual role. This is specially true for the flowering plants, because the flowers they produce are simply their sexual organs dressed up, coloured and often scented to appeal to pollinators: bees, flies, moths, butterflies, beetles, even birds – anything that can crawl or fly and, attracted first by the sight and smell of the flowers and then by the more tangible rewards of tasty nectar and pollen, earn its keep by bringing about fertilization.

Sometimes the first sign of adolescence is unruly behaviour. A plant that started life neat and tidy in its appearance becomes scruffy and unkempt and begins to sprawl about the place. Some plants continue to sprawl all their lives, spreading outwards and rooting as they grow, till they form a thick mat of stems and leaves; among them are many of the most valuable plants for ground cover. The only snag is that some are such hearty growers that you have to watch out that they do not overwhelm less robust plants.

The plants we are concerned with here, however, are not those which continue like this throughout their lives, but those for which this sort of behaviour is an adolescent phase which they will grow out of one day. Some of the oddest examples of this stage of development are to be found in the southern hemisphere. A number of New Zealand trees and shrubs, known locally as 'mikimiki', after a normal appearance as young seedlings, begin to produce thin, wiry shoots growing horizontally at right angles to the main stem. A mass of such shoots may develop, branching and rebranching, carrying small leaves quite unlike adult ones, and often spines as well, and untidily interlaced as if an unskilled person had tried to weave them together in a hurry.

Protection against insecurity

It is thought that this strange juvenile pattern of behaviour, known as divarication, is really a method of self-protection developed by the plant to help it through a vulnerable and insecure age. In very exposed situations, with nothing to cling to or to offer shelter, it would be highly dangerous for plants without strong roots to grow straight up to adult stature. The first strong wind could tear them out of the ground. On the other hand, to develop a good root system a plant needs plenty of foliage, since nearly all its substance, both above and below ground, is manufactured by the leaves. So to avoid the dangers caused by growing upwards, these devaricating plants have grown sideways instead; and although the leaves are tiny, so that the wind can whistle through them without tearing them, there are enough of them to build the roots until the plant is firmly anchored. Then, with its insecurity conquered, it can abandon its sideways growth and grow up, in every sense of the words.

Some of these strange, tortuous, prostrate shrubs stay that way all their lives. Though they reach full adulthood and are perfectly capable of sexual reproduction, they have a tousled, immature look. One of the weirdest-looking is the wire-netting bush, *Corokia cotoneaster*, a member of the dogwood family from New

Zealand, with twiggy branchlets that look like crumpled wire-netting, adorned with tiny yellow flowers, followed by orange fruits. It is hardy in all but the coldest gardens, and, strategically placed where it is bound to be noticed, makes a good conversation-piece for visitors, who cannot quite believe their eyes when they see it.

Most divaricating plants do change their appearance and habit of growth when they become adult. With shrubs the change may be complete within a few seasons, but with trees it may take much longer. Much depends on the conditions: the more exposed the situation, the more likely the adult stage is to be delayed. The bead tree of India, whose hard, round fruits are polished and used for making necklaces and other ornaments, has a New Zealand relation, *Elaeocarpus hookeranus*, which has been known to remain in this peculiar divaricating state for some sixty years.

An astonishing transformation

Perhaps the most astonishing examples of plants that differ greatly in habit and appearance at different stages of their lives are to be found in the ivy family. The species *Pseudopanax crassifolius* starts life as a seedling with fairly normal-looking leaves, between 1 and 2 inches (2.5–5 cm) long, pointed oval in shape. The plant grows upwards as a straight, unbranched, single shoot, which may reach a height of 10 feet (3 m) and has a stiff, artificial look. As it grows, it puts out new leaves that are quite unlike the first ones, or indeed quite unlike any other leaves on earth. They are incredibly long and narrow, reaching a length of as much as 3 feet (90 cm) but only an inch (2.5 cm) or so broad. To complete the weird picture, these adolescent leaves, which are dark green on the upper surface and purple below, with orange midribs, so that they look like painted metal strips, are held out from the main stem at a downward-pointing angle, so that they look like the spokes of a series of strange umbrellas, one above the other.

This ungainly adolescent stage may last for twenty years or more. Then, if conditions are favourable, the single stem begins to branch, and the branches produce a third type of leaf, no longer simple in outline but with three or five segments. After some time, yet another type of leaf appears, simple again in shape and somewhat like the original infant leaves but longer. These at last are the mature leaves. When sufficient branches carrying this final form of foliage have appeared, a last transformation takes place. The long, strip-like leaves which saw the plant through its drawn-out period of adolescence are thrown down as if they had been cut off with a knife, leaving the main stem quite bare. Relieved of its burden, the stem thickens and hardens and turns ash-grey, finishing like a long pole. At the top of this, the mature branches with their adult leaves are ready at long last to produce clusters of greenish flowers, followed by black fruit.

So completely unlike each other are the different stages of growth that when adolescent and mature specimens were first discovered they were thought to be quite different plants and given separate names. In its final form *Pseudopanax crassifolius* looks like a neat, round-headed mop at the end of a long, straight handle, which may reach as much as 50 feet (15 m) in height. Unfortunately it is only half-hardy in the British Isles and so can only be grown to its full height in mild localities, free from hard frosts and biting winds. However, if you have a cool greenhouse with a fair amount of room you can try growing the adolescent form in a pot; the extraordinary development and almost incredible leaves will amaze everybody who sees it.

GROWING TO ADULTHOOD

We have dealt with some of the more spectacular examples of the differences in growth, form and habit between the infantile, adolescent and adult stages of plant development. Many others, though not so bizarre in their adolescent state, have very marked differences between their youthful and adult conditions.

Eucalyptus

There are over 500 species of eucalyptus, nearly all of them native to Australia, and they lead a remarkable double life. Most trees throughout the world belong to one of two groups: those with leaves arranged in opposite pairs along the shoots, like the ash and the maple, and those with leaves arranged alternately, like the oak and the elm. The difference between the two groups is so clear and fundamental that botanists use it as one of the simplest means of identification.

The eucalyptus manages to have both opposite and alternate leaves on the same tree. A typical example is *Eucalyptus gunnii*, which is not only one of the most beautiful but also one of the hardiest; its outstanding qualities earned it an Award of Merit from the Royal Horticultural Society in 1950, and it is perhaps the species most often to be found on sale at nurseries and garden centres. Its youthful round leaves are borne in opposite pairs and look like large, flat, silvery coins. They continue in this way for several years, during which the young trees grow rapidly; the round foliage, glinting silver in the sunlight, makes a breathtaking sight. The years of youth pass and then something strange happens. A new type of shoot begins to appear, rather lanky in growth and bearing completely different leaves. Not only are they sickle-shaped instead of round, and sage-green instead of silver, but they are borne alternately instead of in opposite pairs. If allowed to grow unchecked, the cider gum, as *Eucalyptus gunnii* is commonly called, will very soon become a tall, handsome tree. In its native habitat in Tasmania and South Australia it reaches a height of 100 feet (30 m) or more, the lanky shoots bearing the alternate adult leaves elongating still further and carrying clusters of white flowers. Because of its very rapid growth and tall, spreading habit, the cider gum needs plenty of space. So if you buy one in a small pot on impulse at a garden centre, attracted by its round, silvery juvenile foilage, and then, reading on the label that it is hardy, plant it out in the garden, you might be in for a shock when it not only changes its leaf-style but also changes its life-style, shooting up and spreading out and generally taking possession of its surroundings. You may curse it, and wonder whether to root it up or to move house. You need not do either. You can keep it down to size by pruning it regularly into the shape of a bush, thereby retaining the sparkling juvenile leaves – and at the same time providing yourself and your friends with a regular supply of beautiful silvery foliage for house decoration.

The Wattles

A sexual deviation that we have not dealt with before can be seen in that delicately beautiful shrub with feathery leaves and masses of deliciously scented yellow flowers, known to Australians in its homeland as 'wattle', to flower-sellers as 'mimosa', and to botanists as *Acacia* (not on any account to be confused with the thorny tree commonly called by that name, which is a North American native rather confusingly called *Robinia* by botanists). Many of the 500 or more different kinds go through just the same sorts of change from youth to adulthood as we have seen with eucalyptus and others, but sometimes in a more dramatic way; the juvenile leaves, which are feathery in appearance and made up of a large number of small leaflets, give way as maturity approaches to strange-looking expansions of the leaf-stalk called phyllodes, which flatten and become like narrow ribbons, varying in length from less than a inch (2.5 cm) to over a foot (30 cm); and the bunched masses of tiny flowers grow from where these phyllodes join the by now adult. Several species, however, never reach this mature stage but continue to produce only the feathery, juvenile type of leaves. But – and this is the remarkable thing – these species still succeed, despite their youthful appearance, in producing an abundance of flowers among the juvenile leaves.

Most of these precocious youngsters are rather tender, coming as they do from the warmer parts of Australia (there are even one or two species native to Africa). However, the extremely beautiful silver wattle, whose botanical name is *Acacia dealbata*, comes from as far south as Tasmania and so is very nearly hardy in all but the most savage winters. Planted against a sheltered wall, it will make a large shrub or even a small tree. Its angled shoots, white with down, carry silvery, fern-like juvenile leaves, split into as many as twenty divisions, each split again into some fifty tiny leaflets. It makes a magnificent sight, the silvery white foliage setting off the large, round heads of fragrant, golden flowers which appear in the cheerless days of late winter, and which fully entitle the plant to the First Class Certificate awarded to it by the Royal Horticultural Society in 1971. It can grow up to 50 feet (15 m) in height in really favourable places (it regularly reaches 100 feet (30 m) in its native land), but it can easily be kept trimmed, since it not only does not seem to resent being cut but actually appears to enjoy it; and you can usually find a ready market for a bunch or two of flowering shoots at a local flower shop, where they will sell it, at rather more than they paid you, as 'mimosa'.

Common ivy

Perhaps the most widespread example of the striking changes that can occur between the youngster and the adult in northern lands is the common ivy, whose home territory extends from the shores of the Mediterranean through the whole of western Europe, including the British Isles, north to Scandinavia, across the Baltic Sea, down through Estonia and Latvia, and then south across Russia to the Black Sea. Its botanical name is *Hedera helix* and it has a very large number of varieties, ranging from those with small, narrow, sharply pointed leaves, which make admirable pot plants, to broad-leaved ones, sometimes edged or splashed with silver, gold or purple. All these varieties have one thing in common: when they are young they behave in a very shy manner. They like to keep to dark, shady places, and try to avoid open ground; this is because they are heliophobic, i.e. they have a strong aversion to sunlight. While in this state they produce the characteristic juvenile leaves by which the plant is known, called by most of us simply 'ivy-shaped', and by botanists 'palmate'.

During its youth the ivy runs along the ground by means of rapidly growing shoots bearing the well-known juvenile leaves and capable of forming fresh roots anywhere along their entire length; these dig themselves into the ground at any suitable place, new running shoots appear, and within a short time a shady spot may be completely covered with a carpet of ivy. This youthful stage may be prolonged indefinitely, till one day a shoot, pushing outwards to explore new territory, and always avoiding the sun, comes to something – a tree, a shady wall, an outbuilding, a garden shed – with a vertical surface up which it can climb. The plant is nearing its goal. Stimulated by touch, the exploring shoot undergoes certain changes which initiate its period of adolescence. The stem thickens and flattens, gathering the structural strength it needs to start it climbing. The roots it sends out change their character entirely; they are no longer needed for feeding but for hugging. In fact they have ceased to be true roots at all and have turned into grippers whose job it is to bind the stem tightly to the 'host' during its upward climb.

These grasping roots have the same aversion to sunlight as the young shoots, so the climbing stem remains in the shade. And so the ivy continues to grow upwards, not perhaps quite as fast as it did in infancy, when it was running about on the ground, but at a steady pace of maybe a foot (30 cm) or so a year, producing the same hand-shaped juvenile leaves. This adolescent behaviour lasts for a long time – ten years is often said to be the minimum length for this stage of development – and then something remarkable happens. In spite of its dislike of strong light, which has caused it to lead a sheltered existence for so many years, the plant is touched one day by the sun's rays. Maybe it has reached the highest branches of the tree, or the top of the wall, and can hide no longer, or perhaps the tree on which it is growing has dropped its leaves in the autumn, exposing the ivy suddenly to full light.

Whatever the cause, those rays of sunshine have a very power-ful effect. The top of the plant, which until now has done everything to avoid the sun, now eagerly seeks it; instead of being heliophobic it has become heliotropic, or sun-seeking. While the lower leaves, still in the shade, remain in their juvenile state, the sun-struck tip of the stem starts to grow upwards and outwards, exposing itself to all the sunlight it can get and no longer clinging by roots to its support. Its branches become thicker and harder, and bear quite a different type of leaf, not at all like the attractively lobed juvenile foliage but whole and undivided, coarser and rather boring in appearance. These are the adult branches, and in late autumn they bear clustered heads of yellowish green flowers, followed by dull black berries. Another odd thing is that, while the juvenile part of the plant is evergreen, the adult branches drop their leaves after fruiting.

As a matter of interest, if cuttings from the adult branches can be persuaded to root they will remain entirely adult, and can be grown as upright shrubs, flowering and fruiting in abundance each year. It is unlikely that anyone would want to do so, except out of curiosity, since the juveniles are so much more attractive than the adults. It does serve to remind us, however, how impor-tant it is to choose the right part of the plant if we want to propagate it.

Immature adults

We have seen how most things grow from immaturity to maturity, often with remarkable changes of appearance and personality; how some fail to break out of their juvenile state, either because of the treatment they receive or because they have somehow lost the capacity to grow up; how one or two even manage to remain juvenile in appearance and yet to achieve sexual maturity. The one kind of plant we have not yet dealt with is one that shows every sign of having reached full adulthood in its leaves, stems and habit of growth, and yet lacks the most important feature of all, the thing to which all the changes from immaturity to maturity are normally supposed to lead – namely sexual capability.

Some plants of this kind bear what look like perfect flowers, fully equipped with male and female sexual organs. They may even produce what look like seeds but are really tiny buds, giving rise to 'seedlings' which are not new individuals resulting from sexual union but really just parts of the parent plant. They represent what might be called 'virgin birth', a form of what is scientifically called *apomixis*, from the Greek for 'without intercourse'. A very common example is the ordinary dandelion, a group of species known botanically as *Taraxacum officinale*, which although visited by a large assortment of crawling and flying insects is never fertilized by them because the flowers have become impotent.

Many garden flowers have been made sterile by the work of plant-breeders, particularly double flowers, in many of which the male organs or the female organs or both have been aborted and turned into extra petals. These, of course, have to be propagated by cuttings or division or some similar vegetative means.

Adults that never flower

Some very useful plants for the gardener are those that have fully adult foliage but never produce any flowers at all, sterile or otherwise. The act of flowering is often accompanied by a spurt in growth, so that the flowering shoots become long and straggly, and the plant loses its compact appearance. Sometimes, even though all the other stems become lanky and produce flowers, one will remain short and stocky and fail to behave like the rest. If this flowerless stem is cut off and made to root in a propagating frame, or pegged down and coaxed into rooting while still attached to the parent plant, and then cut off and planted separately, it may retain its inability to flower indefinitely.

In very many garden plants this failure to bloom would be

highly undesirable, since often the chief reason we grow a plant is to get flowers. With herbs, though, what we want is leaves rather than blossom, so the flowerless state may be a definite advantage. Already several varieties are on sale which have been propagated from sterile shoots in this way. They may be hard to find, and they may cost more money, but they are worth it.

There are non-flowering varieties of sage, for instance, which are much superior to the usual flowering ones for the herb garden; the growth is neater and more compact, and the leaves have a better, more aromatic flavour. It seems as if the strength which would otherwise have gone into producing flowers has gone instead into making the leaves tastier.

The old-fashioned camomile lawn, dating back to Tudor times and before, and giving off a delicious (and reputedly aphrodisiac) scent when trodden on in the warm summer days, does not usually come up to the expectations aroused by the romantic writings of gardening journalists. The trouble is that if you try to grow such a lawn from ordinary plants you find that when it starts to flower it becomes straggly and unattractive. Bare patches appear, and far from walking about on the lawn and savouring its aromatic scent you keep off it, and order others to do so too, to try to prevent it from becoming entirely threadbare. However, several years ago a gardener noticed a plant with a shoot on it that never flowered. The shoot was rooted, cut off and planted separately, and found to retain its flowerless habit. From that original plant thousands more have now been produced. Lawns planted with that variety are now to be found in gardens all over the country. They never flower, and so they never get straggly or threadbare, but make a dense mass of foliage like a thick green pile carpet.

There is scope here for the observant amateur gardener. If you discover a non-flowering shoot among your herbs, and when you propagate it the resulting plants retain the non-flowering habit, you may be on to something good. Not only do flowering stems tend to become leggy and untidy, but they usually bear, below the flowers, a reduced form of leaf called a bract, which is narrow, often hard and sometimes scaly, and not much use for flavouring. How rewarding it might be, both in satisfaction and perhaps in money, to produce a good, compact, leafy variety of thyme, say, or marjoram, devoid of flowers and the nuisance they cause.

Now to summarize the practical lessons for the gardener from our exploration of some of the changes experienced by plants in their progress from infancy to maturity:

1 Use your imagination. When choosing plants that you are going to live with for some time, particularly trees and shrubs, try to imagine how they will behave at the different stages of life as they grow and develop. If what you want is too big for the space available, choose something smaller.

2 If you set your heart on a certain plant for the charm of its juvenile foliage, and you therefore want to keep it immature, start cutting it back regularly from the beginning.

3 Instead of buying plants which call for constant clipping to keep them the way you want them, think about choosing one or two of the 'permanent juveniles', which need no effort on your part to prevent them from growing up.

4 Keep your eyes open. There is always the exciting possibility of finding a variety which, by being fixed at some particular stage of development, shows attractive characteristics.

CHAPTER EIGHT

Feeding and sleep

THE NATURAL WAY

FEW THINGS rouse such heated argument as the subject of feeding. Advocates of what they call 'natural'methods argue that Mother Earth provides everything a plant needs for health, happiness and self-fulfilment; artificial feeding is not only unnatural and unnecessary, but unhealthy as well. Believers in this doctrine tend to call themselves 'organic' gardeners. Those who do not share their simple faith call them less complimentary things, like muck-and-mystery merchants. The more extreme believers in muck-and-mystery form themselves into sects, and argue amongst themselves about what is 'natural' and what is 'unnatural'.

Some are really in it for the money, and manage to sell gullible gardeners all sorts of dubious (and high-priced) stuff offering back-to-nature promises. Most, though, are simply sincere fanatics. There may well be some truth in what they say, but their assertions go way beyond the ascertainable facts. Unfortunately their views get so much publicity that many sensible people are made to feel guilty when they give a plant a dose of much-needed fertilizer from a packet.

The law of return

It is true that if we put back into the soil everything a plant had taken out of it, then there might be no need for any other food. After all the natural cycle, established over vast stretches of time, consists of the return to the earth, sooner or later, of every plant and animal that has ever lived upon it, and of all the waste material it has produced in the course of its life. Biologists call it the law of return. It may work in the jungle, but it certainly cannot be relied on in our gardens.

We constantly take more plant material from our gardens than we put back. If we grow vegetables or fruit, we eat the produce, and that means a loss to the soil in which it grew. True, we can put all the waste – the vegetable trimmings, the peelings, the apple cores and so on – on the compost heap, where it turns into a very useful soil conditioner; but much of what we eat is burned up by us in the course of our activities, and if we have inside sanitation we do not return to the soil the vegetable residues that have passed through us. Some people say that the water-closet was the most disastrous invention of our civilization: our human wastes, rich in plant foods, had always been returned to the soil, to restore fertility and grow splendid crops; now they go down the drains and along the sewers, and finish up by polluting our waterways instead of fertilizing our plants. This may be all very true, but it is of no practical help to us as things are at present – though perhaps one day, when the human race has plundered the earth to such an extent that resources are running dangerously low, our present sewage systems will have to be scrapped, and quite different methods invented – or re-invented – to recycle our body wastes and give them back to the land.

Some enlightened local authorities nowadays offer sewage sludge in a fairly pleasant (or at any rate not too unpleasant) form to commercial growers. A few can even arrange to supply it to gardeners, who may, if it has been properly treated, find it useful as a soil conditioner. Before you buy any ask for an analysis of it, particularly of any toxic substances it might contain. However useful it may be as a soil improver, though, sewage sludge is likely at best to be poor in food value for plants, because a great many of the soluble nutrients will have been washed away during processing.

With things we grow in the garden it is possible to put back in the soil much of what they have taken out of it. Careful gathering and composting of fallen leaves, lawn mowings, prunings and dead flowers will give us valuable material for digging in or spreading on the ground as a mulch (see pages 38–40). But it is almost impossible to return everything: every time you cut a bunch of flowers to give to a friend something is lost.

What is 'organic'?

We have seen that advocates of 'natural' as opposed to 'artificial' gardening tend to call the system they preach 'organic'. The organic movement crusades even more strongly against the use of artificial chemicals for killing pests and controlling disease than against artificial fertilizers. Its adherents seem to suggest that no pests or diseases ever attacked our crops (or for that matter ourselves) till the dreaded artificial fertilizers came along. These views are a perfectly reasonable reaction against the almost indiscriminate use of poisonous sprays and dusts, which have done so much damage to wild life, both vegetable and animal. All sensible people would like to see the use of poisonous substances kept to a minimum, and for alerting us to the dangers we must be grateful to the champions of organic methods.

All the same, such champions have put themselves in a some-what silly position by their use of the word 'organic' to mean everything they consider good. Some of the most dangerous of all pesticides are, in the chemical sense, organic. The two chief groups are the organochlorines (which include the highly toxic DDT, so dangerous that it is no longer available to the amateur gardener in many countries) and the organophosphorus compounds, which must not be used by some sensitive people because of the devastating effect on the nervous system. Both these groups consist of carbon compounds, in the one case combined with chlorine and in the other with phosphorus, so they are chemically defined as organic. Yet these would probably be put at the top of the list of most hated chemicals by advocates of 'organic' methods. The confusion arises because the word organic was once used to mean substances produced by living organisms, both animal and vegetable. The word has long since ceased to have that meaning, chemically speaking, so it is high time the champions of 'natural' methods abandoned its use.

WHAT FOODS DO PLANTS NEED?

The chief supply of food for the growing plant comes not from the soil but from the air. By a process known as photosynthesis the green colouring matter of plants, called chlorophyll, uses the energy provided by sunlight to convert the carbon dioxide in the air we breathe, together with water, into the sugars and starches that form the main substance from which the plant is built up. During the process, oxygen is given off into the air.

Although the bulk of the plant's substance is built up from air and water, certain other chemicals are needed too. These are normally taken up by the roots, and are what gardeners usually refer to as plant foods. To be taken in by its roots, these foods must be completely dissolved in water. Insoluble substances in the soil are no use to a plant as food – though some of them may be gradually broken down and made soluble by tiny organisms in the soil, or by secretions from the roots themselves. The soil also has to be in the right condition to hold on to the dissolved food till it is needed by the roots; otherwise, being so soluble, it will be washed away by rain.

The nutrient salts are simple chemicals, no matter how complex the substance they came from may be; to a plant's feeding roots, which suck the liquid in, the dissolved salt is exactly the same whether it came from a smelly manure heap or from odourless crystals in a packet.

The elements needed

Of the ninety or so different chemical elements known to exist in nature, it is generally agreed that at least a dozen are needed by plants, the amount of each required varying according to the kind of plant, the time of year and the stage of growth.

None of the twelve is needed in vast quantities; indeed, too much can do more harm than good, like overfeeding a baby. Six are needed in relatively large amounts, and are known as the major elements, and six are needed in much smaller quantities and are known as the minor elements.

The major elements (with their chemical symbols) are: Nitrogen (N), Phosphorus (P), Potassium (K), Magnesium (Mg), Calcium (Ca) and Sulphur (S). The minor elements are: Iron (Fe), Manganese (Mn), Boron (B), Copper (Cu), Zinc (Zn) and Molybdenum (Mo).

In addition, minute amounts of certain other elements are needed by some plants, though not necessarily by all. These include sodium, chlorine and silicon, and are often referred to as trace elements – a name commonly used also to include those we have called minor elements.

It is important to realize that the distinction drawn between major and minor elements only refers to the quantities needed by the plant; the minor elements, however small the amount needed may be, are just as vital as the major ones. Without them plants die.

Luckily it is extremely rare to find any normal soil lacking in the minor elements, particularly if it is kept reasonably well supplied with humus-forming materials. Research scientists working in laboratories where they grow plants in chemical solutions have managed to produce deficiency symptoms by leaving out one or more of the required elements, but even then only by using highly purified chemicals. The reason is that ordinary grades usually contain impurities, which most likely include minute amounts of the other chemicals the plant requires. If such impurities are found even in normal, comparatively refined laboratory chemicals, they are almost certain to be found, in greater amounts still, not only in the soil, which is a rich mixture of all kinds of minerals and other things, but in commercial fertilizers too.

In fact, laboratory workers are much more able to produce unhealthy symptoms in a plant by giving it too much of a chemical than by giving it too little. And such symptoms will be not only those of poisoning through excess but also of deficiency brought about by the fact that too much of one thing will, as we shall see, often lead to the 'locking up' of another, so that the plant can no longer take it in.

The moral is that plants, like people, can have too much of a good thing. So never mess about applying chemicals in order to remedy a supposed shortage of trace elements. You are almost certain to do more harm than good. If you are really convinced, from a plant's symptoms, that there is a deficiency, call in an expert. He will most likely find that there is no deficiency, and that something else is wrong.

Plants can usually get their requirements, as and when they need them, from the soil, provided that it is reasonably fertile. Fertilizers should only be given by the gardener when the plant can make use of them; given at other times they can damage, or even poison, the roots. Only by watching a plant's progress and observing weather and soil conditions can you tell if and when to feed it. Do not, therefore, take too seriously the instructions given in gardening calendars and magazines as to what you should do and when, week by week or even day by day.

HOW MUCH SLEEP?

Feeding times are naturally governed to a large extent by sleeping times.

Two types of sleep are recognized in plants. The first is the response to the daily rhythm of light and darkness, which in some species has a striking effect. Flowers may close at night, and sometimes droop as well; leaves may fold up, and leaf-stalks flatten themselves tightly against the stem. In some cases the plant seems to collapse completely, almost as if it was terrified of the dark. The most remarkable example is probably the sensitive plant, *Mimosa sensitiva*, or its even more sensitive close relative the humble plant, *Mimosa pudica*. A member of the pea family from tropical America, it can easily be raised from seed in a greenhouse, where it will make quite a good-sized plant in a 4-inch (10 cm) pot, bearing rather inconspicuous heads of rose-purple flowers in the summer, resembling those of the clover. The spectacular feature is the leaves, which are made up of a number of leaflets arranged in pairs along a central stalk. As dusk approaches, you can watch the pairs of leaflets close themselves tightly together. Next morning, when the light returns, the stalks lift themselves up and the leaves open themselves out, just as if nothing had happened. But the really extraordinary thing is that, even in broad daylight, if you touch the leaves, or even blow on them sharply, they will instantly fold up and collapse; it is the nearest thing to a sudden sign of alarm in the plant world. A direct hit by a drop of rain will trigger the same instant reaction.

These movements are not fully understood, but they seem to be an expression of the need for protection from cold during the night – and in the case of the sensitive plant from sudden damage during the day. Huddling down during cold nights is seen in many flowers, such as those of the carrot and the pansy. Even some plants that show no sign of such sleep movements when they are grown up do so in their early infancy, when they are at their most helpless: the seed-leaves of young cucumbers, for instance, can be seen to close together in the cold night hours and open up in the morning, even though their later leaves stay open day and night. By presenting a smaller surface area to the night air, the young plants stand less risk of losing much-needed heat.

How sleep affects growing up

A less obvious but vitally important aspect of the amount of rest a plant gets at night is its effect on the process of growing up. As far as flowering plants are concerned, the adult state is reached when blossoming takes place (see chapter 7). Some plants need a long night's sleep before they can start to produce flower-buds; others cannot make it unless they have short nights. It is the night length that matters rather than the day length, as research workers have shown by experiments in which in some cases they interrupted the plants' period of darkness by brief exposure to bright light, and in other cases they interrupted the period of daylight with dark spells. The plants that had their waking hours disturbed kept to their normal pattern of flowering, but those whose nights were disturbed became completely disorganized, and if the treatment was prolonged failed to flower at all.

The reasons for this are too many and too complicated to go into fully here. One important factor is the matter of breathing. When people go to sleep, they go on breathing in the same way as during the day, taking in oxygen and giving out carbon dioxide – though they slow down a bit, and maybe snore. With plants, things are different. As we have seen, leaves give off oxygen during the day as a result of the process by which they use light and carbon dioxide to build up the plant. Plants breathe too, however, though not so fast as animals, and like animals they use up oxygen and give off carbon dioxide in the process. When darkness comes they continue to breathe, but since there is no light photosynthesis stops; so while darkness lasts they use up oxygen and give out carbon dioxide – the exact opposite of what they did during the day.

The proportions of its time that a plant spends on the different sides of its double life are among the many influences that determine when it should come into flower; in other words whether it is a long-night or a short-night plant. A very important factor in determining when a plant flowers is the latitude of its country of origin. At the equator night and day are equal in length all the year round, so neither long-night nor short-night plants would ever stand a chance of coming into flower there. As we go north or south from the equator, so the lengths of day and night vary more and more according to the seasons, till in the polar regions there is almost continuous daylight in the summer and almost continuous darkness in the winter.

It is adaptation to these varying conditions that has given rise to the existence of long-night and short-night plants. Chrysanthemums, for instance, will not produce flower-buds unless they have long nights. Study of the effects of different day and night lengths on the growth and flowering of plants, known as *photoperiodism*, has only been carried out within recent years. Before this people had long been puzzled as to why a certain plant would always bloom at roughly the same time each year, though the weather might be hot and dry one year and cold and wet another; now it is realized that the one absolutely predictable and unvarying thing about any given date, year after year, is its day length.

As a result of the study of photoperiodism, growers have been able to create whole new industries, by artificially lengthening or shortening the amount of light and darkness a plant receives, and so coaxing it into flower at will. The marvellous modern all-the-year-round chrysanthemum, obtainable from flower shops, and smothered in blossom at any season, is thus a product of modern technology.

How much rest?

In addition to this day-by-day pattern of sleep and waking, there is also a yearly rhythm, sometimes also called sleep and waking but perhaps better described as rest and activity. In nearly every case, at any rate in non-tropical climates, the period of rest occurs during the winter, when temperatures are coldest and days shortest; even plants that flower in the winter are simply opening the blossom-buds already formed during the preceding warmer weather when growth and activity took place. Deciduous trees and shrubs drop their leaves and hibernate, because if their leaves remained on extra energy would be needed to enable them to battle against the cold, yet shortage of light makes considerably less energy available.

Herbaceous plants die right down to the ground, and keep their remaining underground parts from freezing to death by means of their covering of earth, supplemented by the dead leaves and stems they have provided themselves with for their extra protection, and in the harshest weather, if they are lucky, a welcome additional blanket of snow. Annuals die completely, right to the ends of their roots, and exist through the winter as seeds.

The very last thing any living creature, whether plant or animal, wants when it is trying to rest is to have food forced upon it. This is particularly so with nitrogenous fertilizers, especially in the quick-acting nitrate form, which if applied to the garden in winter might during a mild spell stimulate premature growth, and which in any case, being readily soluble, will probably be washed out of the soil and wasted. In fact such fertilizers should not be given in the autumn either, because they will only lead to soft, flabby growth, which is likely to be severely damaged by the first hard spell of winter weather.

Salts of the other nutrient elements needed are not on the whole so easily washed away, provided that the ground is in the right condition to hold them. Indeed, if you use 'single fertilizers' (that is, those that supply only one of the necessary elements) it could be a good idea to apply a potassium fertilizer in late autumn before digging begins, especially in the vegetable garden. Most gardeners, however, use ready-mixed fertilizers, and since these contain nitrogen it would, as we have just seen, probably be harmful and certainly wasteful to use them at this time of year.

The most sensible general rule, therefore, is to apply bulky stuff such as manure, compost, peat and the other 'soil improvers' in late autumn, and mineral fertilizers – commonly and meaninglessly called 'artificials' – in the spring and summer. In that way you will get the best of both worlds.

SWEET OR SOUR?

Before we go into the matter of what plant foods are available and how to use them, we must spend some time examining the subject of soil acidity. The degree of alkalinity or acidity – often called 'sweetness' and 'sourness' – in the soil has a very important effect on what happens to the nutrients in it and whether a plant growing in it thrives or not.

Plants differ considerably in their preferences. Some of the choosiest are those that refuse to grow in anything but acid soils; they are known as 'lime-haters', and include such beautiful plants as rhododendrons and camellias and most, though not all, of the heathers. The reason why they are said to hate lime is that the alkaline soils to which they so strongly object usually contain considerable quantities of calcium, the predominant chemical in lime. Calcium, as we have seen, is one of the major elements needed by plants; it is present in some form in most normal soils, but if it is not in the right proportion it can cause trouble. The more calcium there is, usually in the form of limestone particles or chalk, the more alkaline (or 'sweet') the soil becomes; the less there is the more acid (or 'sour') the soil. For most garden plants something between the two extremes is best. Luckily there is a quick and simple way to check your soil.

The pH scale

The acidity or alkalinity of soil – or rather, to be strictly accurate, of the soil water – is usually measured by what is known as its pH. The meaning of those letters is rather technical,* and need not concern us here. Theoretically the pH ranges from 0, representing extreme acidity, to 14, representing extreme alkalinity. The mid-point on the scale, 7, is neutral, indicating a condition neither acid nor alkaline. In practice, you will never find anything like either extreme, since values normally do not go much above or below 7. Because of its effect on pH, calcium has an importance far beyond that of merely being a necessary element of nutrition, since the acidity or alkalinity of the soil strongly influences the ability of a plant to take up other nutrients as well.

With certain exceptions, already briefly mentioned and dealt with in more detail later, most garden plants do best in a slightly acid soil with a pH value of about 6.5. If your soil is at this pH level, you can consider yourself lucky; if not, treatment is needed.

The acid test

Professional growers, whose livelihood depends on highly accurate soil analysis, use elaborate and expensive pH meters to measure acidity, or else they get the job done for them by outside contractors. Amateurs can buy cheap and easy kits for the purpose, which give accurate enough results for the needs of the

---

*If you are interested, it relates to the hydrogen ion concentration.

average gardener. Such kits include a glass phial or test-tube, a bottle of indicator solution and a colour chart; all you have to do is to shake some samples of soil up with distilled water (tap water is no use because it will have its own probably high pH, which will influence the result), add a few drops of the indicator solution, watch the colour change and compare it with the colours on the chart. Against each of these is printed a figure, and the one against the colour that most closely matches that of the solution gives the pH of the soil.

A simpler and even cheaper method, not quite so accurate but good enough for most purposes, is to use an indicator paper, which is a kind of litmus paper sold in booklets containing several narrow strips. As before, samples of soil are shaken up with water, and one of the strips is dipped into the solution. The strip changes colour, and this is compared with a series of colours printed inside the cover of the booklet to find the pH value.

How to reduce acidity

To raise the pH figure of a too acid soil to the required level of 6.5, some form of lime should be added. Quicklime (calcium oxide), which is obtained by burning limestone or chalk in kilns, is the most concentrated, but its use is not to be recommended because it is very caustic in its action. Slaked or hydrated lime (calcium hydroxide) may be bought at horticultural suppliers or garden centres as a fine white powder. It is not so quick-acting as quicklime, but it is much pleasanter to handle and, being non-caustic, has no scorching action on plants if by accident some drops on them. For fairly rapid results, especially in the vegetable garden, it can be useful. However, the best form for general use in gardens – and in potting composts – is calcium carbonate, which can be bought as ground limestone or, in finer powder still, as chalk.

The type of soil makes a considerable difference both to the initial pH value and to the amount of chalk needed to change that pH to the required 6.5, as shown in the table overleaf:

Chalk needed to bring soil to pH 6.5 (per sq. yard/sq. metre)					
Present pH:	6.0	5.5	5.0	4.5	4.0
Acidity:	slight	moderate	marked	strong	very strong
Soil:	lb/kg	lb/kg	lb/kg	lb/kg	lb/kg
Stony/sandy	½/0.25	1/0.45	1½/0.70	2/0.90	2½/1.15
Loamy	¾/0.35	1½/0.70	2¼/1.0	3/1.35	4/1.80
Clay	1/0.45	2/0.90	3/1.35	4/1.80	5/2.25
Peaty	1¼/0.60	2½/1.15	3¾/1.70	5/2.25	6/2.75

Note: If hydrated lime is used instead of chalk, give half the above rates

How to reduce alkalinity

It is much more difficult to reduce the pH of a very limy soil. Applying acid peat can help, especially moss peat, but the higher the pH of the soil the more peat will be needed, and the dressing may well have to be repeated every year.

A further way to reduce pH in some soils is to use flowers of sulphur before planting. By the action of moisture and soil organisms, this is transformed into a dilute solution of sulphuric acid, which can lower the pH quite rapidly. The usual recommended rate of application is ½lb per square yard (250g per square metre), but besides being cripplingly expensive such a dose would be unnecessarily large for anything but very alkaline soils with a pH of around 8.5 to 9. For soils with a pH of 7 to 8 or a little more, 4oz per square yard (125g per square metre) should be quite enough. Ferrous sulphate, applied at the same rate, has also proved useful in remedying alkaline conditions.

It must be remembered, though, that the effects of these treatments do not usually last very long; the natural pH of the soil keeps trying to reassert itself. The treatment will therefore have to be repeated when the testing kit shows that the soil is reverting to type.

When to correct the pH balance

On the whole, the effects of liming to correct acidity last longer than those of applying sulphur to correct alkalinity. So it is normally best to apply lime before autumn digging, to give it time to work (and to avoid possible damage to plants), and sulphur shortly before sowing or planting in the spring. If peat is to be dug in, autumn is usually the most convenient time to do so, but it is often a good idea to mix some with the soil in the hole when planting, and more can be used later as a mulch (see page 38).

Indigestion in plants

As we have seen, most garden plants thrive in slightly acid soil with a pH of about 6.5. However, some are happier with more alkaline soils, with a pH reading above 7, and some with acid soils, with a pH of 6 or lower. It is important, therefore, to know if any of the plants you want to grow come within these choosy types, so that you can give them the conditions they like.

With human beings, indigestion most frequently comes from too much acid. With plants, indigestion – that is, failure to take in and utilize food properly – is more likely to occur because the soil is too alkaline. The problem is to strike the right dietary balance, because excess of one thing often leads to deficiency of another. In acid soils, for instance, a deficiency of calcium and molybdenum can occur. At the other end of the scale, in alkaline soils some other essential elements are made insoluble, particularly iron and manganese, and usually boron too. They are said to be 'locked up', and plants with a specially high need for them are, as we shall see, starved to death unless something is done to remedy the situation.

Lime-lovers

On the whole, these are fairly easy-going. It is not so much that they demand a high proportion of lime in the soil as that they are prepared to put up with it. There is a common belief that all vegetables are lime-lovers; as a result, many gardeners subject their vegetable patches to heavy dressings of lime every year as a kind of religious ritual, without ever measuring the pH to see whether liming is necessary, and very often with detrimental results to certain crops.

The fact of the matter is that most vegetables prefer a slightly acid soil, like most other garden plants. Careful scientific research over the last quarter of a century, during which thousands of crops have been grown and studied, has proved this beyond a doubt. The National Vegetable Research Station has published its findings on the subject, and these should clear the matter up once and for all.

Briefly, what has been discovered is that most vegetables are happy with pH values ranging from as low as 5.5 (moderately acid) to 7 (neutral). These include: beans, Brussels sprouts, cabbages, cucumbers, marrows (squashes), parsley, parsnips, peas, radishes, swedes, sweet corn, tomatoes and turnips. In fact an even more acid soil, with a pH between 5 and 6, is best for that very important vegetable, the potato, to get the best quality and the highest yield.

Among those vegetables that do well in soil with somewhat higher pH values, ranging from 6.5 (slightly acid) to 7.5 (slightly alkaline), are asparagus, beetroot, carrot, cauliflower, celery, lettuce, onion, leek, and spinach.

Why is it, then, that vegetables have the reputation of demanding regular liming of the soil? The answer is probably that, because more is removed from the vegetable plot than from other parts of the garden, and therefore more fertilizers are added to the soil to replace what is lost, there is a tendency for perhaps most types of soil to become more acid in the process. It is therefore a good idea to check the pH every year, taking samples of soil from different parts of the vegetable garden, since the pH can vary from place to place, and if the reading is below 6 to apply chalk or lime as shown in the table on page 128. (If club-root disease attacks crops of the cabbage family in your garden, it is perhaps best to raise the pH of the soil in which they are to be grown to the neutral point of 7, since the fungus that causes the disease thrives in acid conditions.)

Turning from vegetables, we find one or two species of plant in the rest of the garden that really do seem to revel in limy conditions. Clematis, for instance, never seems to be truly happy unless the soil in which it is growing has a fairly high pH value. Other beautiful things that do well in limy ground are the peony species and hybrids, both herbaceous and shrubby, and all the varieties of the hardy shrub *Hibiscus syriacus*, together with the many different kinds of *Hypericum* (St John's-wort).

Limy ground is really of two different kinds. In one, the soil, which may be quite deep, contains a good deal of chalk, such as the yellow, sticky substance known as marl, in which the lime is mixed with heavy clay. The second kind consists of a rather shallow layer of soil over more or less solid chalk.

Lime-haters

Unlike the lime-lovers, most of which are really just lime-tolerant rather than dependent on it, the lime-haters simply cannot stand it; the slightest trace of free lime or chalk in the soil is liable to make the leaves turn yellow and sickly. The plant makes miserable growth (or stops growing altogether); the leaves, lacking chlorophyll, drop prematurely, and unless something is done to remedy the situation the plant dies – or lingers on in such a wretched state that it would be kinder to put it out of its misery by pulling it up and putting it on the bonfire. In the most extreme cases of lime intolerance, the plant may simply refuse to put out any roots at all rather than let them so much as touch the offending lime.

It used to be thought that for some reason such plants just hated lime, and that was all there was to it. Now it is known that the real trouble is not that lime is poisonous to these so-called 'calcifuge' plants, but that its presence above a certain level affects the availability of some vital plant foods. While lime actually helps to make nitrogen and phosphorus more readily available, it has the opposite effect on some other elements, notably iron and manganese. The lime-hating plants, having both a high need for those elements and a low ability to extract them from the soil, cannot cope with such conditions and become sick.

In the old days, rich landowners with limy ground would have tons of it carted away and replaced with lime-free soil, so that they could grow calcifuge plants and thus be one-up on neighbouring landowners. Nowadays one does not have to go to those lengths. Chemicals of a type known as sequestrols, which can be bought under various trade names from garden suppliers, contain iron and manganese in a form that is not made insoluble by lime and so can be taken up by the plant's roots without any difficulty. The snag with sequestrols is that because they have been made so soluble for the benefit of lime-hating plants they are easily washed away, so the dose has to be repeated over and over again. Unless you have endless time, patience and money, therefore, it is not very sensible to try to defy nature in this way. Gardening is quite enough of a struggle against nature in any case, and there are any number of excellent lime-tolerant plants to keep a reasonable gardener happy.

In any case, few of the rich landowners had much success in the end in their attempts to replace limy with lime-free soil. Water rising from the chalky layers below the new soil would bring dissolved calcium salts up with it, and sooner or later the cherished lime-haters would begin to suffer.

We should now turn to the subject of watering, but before we deal with it in general terms this is an opportune moment to mention a peculiarly modern danger concerning the watering of the lime-hating plants. Nowadays nearly every home in the country has mains water laid on. In the old days, water came from a local supply. Maybe it smelt a bit, maybe nowadays it would be declared unfit for human consumption, but because it came from the same district – perhaps even from a well in the same garden – it was likely to have the same pH as the local soil. Now, because our mains water is supplied from a series of vast reservoirs, what comes out of your tap may be very hard – in other words, full of calcium salts – even though the soil in your garden is quite lime-free.

If in a dry spell you use that hard tap-water for lime-hating plants, you will be forcing upon them the very thing they dislike most. And if the dose is repeated, you may begin to build up so much lime that the plants start to show the same symptoms as if the soil had been limy in the first place. It is best to improve the water-holding capacity of your soil (see pages 27–8) before planting, so that watering is not needed, but if it ever should be needed rainwater is much safer than tap-water.

The problem is at its worst with house-plants in pots, which simply have to be watered from time to time. Most of the popular ones are lime-tolerant, so they are perfectly happy with tap-water; but if you get a lime-hating one you could be in trouble. Every Christmas thousands of those colourful, flower-laden pot plants known as Indian azaleas are given as presents. The recipients say

'How beautiful', and then subject them to well-intentioned cruelty by soaking the compost in the pot with tap-water. Being largely
composed of lime-free peat, the compost protects the plant's roots
from the shock for a little while, but after several such waterings
the leaves start turning yellow and soon begin to drop off, along
with the flowers and unopened buds. If you are given one of these
plants and you want to keep it, use rainwater instead of tap-water;
if you have nothing but tap-water; boiling it and using it after it
has cooled down is better than using it straight from the tap.

WATERING

How much water should plants be given, how frequently, and
when? The answer is not by any means a simple one, because so
many factors have to be taken into account: the nature of the plant
itself, its living conditions and its state of growth, the temperature
and humidity both of the soil or compost and of the air, and many
other things besides, including drainage.

Perhaps the most frequent question asked by people when they
buy, or are given, a plant is 'How often should I water it?' Not
only is the question impossible to answer, but the very fact of
asking it shows a completely misguided attitude. Watering at
fixed intervals, irrespective of conditions, is probably responsible
for more misery and death among plants than anything else.

A few general hints can be given, however. The first is that
plants need more water when they are growing than when they are
resting: during growth the leaves are giving off a considerable
amount of water, which needs to be replaced, whereas while a
plant is resting it either loses its leaves or they give off water at a
much reduced rate. In some cases, notably with orchids, strict
withholding of water is necessary during the resting period,
otherwise there will be no flowers.

The second general hint is that soft-wooded and fast-growing
plants need more water than hard-wooded and slow-growing
ones. There are exceptions – for instance most succulents – but in
general the greater the proportion of water a plant is made up of,
the more it needs to keep it going. Besides, hard-wooded trees and
shrubs normally have roots that go down a long way, so that they
can find water below ground even when the surface is dry.

That brings us to the third general hint, which is that when watering is done it must be done thoroughly. Give a good soaking; surface dribbles do more harm than good. The reason is that plants are usually better if they have to do some work for their living; roots are healthier, and can actually take up more water, if they have to search for it a bit. If you provide a readily available supply of water near the surface, the plant will choose the easy way and send out shallow roots to take advantage of the superficial moisture which you have so generously laid on. Then if a drought comes, and you are away on holiday or there are restrictions on watering, the shallow roots, denied their customary ration of water, may shrivel and die.

This principle of always giving a thorough soaking is very important where plants in pots are concerned. Water must get right down to the roots, where it is needed, and the best way to ensure this is to continue till the surplus runs out of the bottom of the pot. With plants in the home, this means standing them in the sink or washbasin, so as not to spoil the furniture; when they have completely drained off, so that no more water runs out, they should be stood in saucers. Do not allow water to accumulate in the saucer; to let the base of the pot stand in the wet is to provide just the conditions for the roots to rot. For certain house-plants, such as the ever-popular African violet (*Saintpaulia*), which like a fair amount of humidity in the air surrounding them, a good way of giving them what they want is to half-fill a saucer or other receptacle with water and then place a good layer of pebbles in it, so that when the pot is standing on these it is clear of the water but the atmosphere around is kept moist.

The fourth general principle, and perhaps the most important one, is that *water should never be given unless it is needed*. A few bog-plants actually thrive on standing in the wet all the time, but that is because their roots have been so modified as to be practically rot-proof, and also to be capable of extracting oxygen from the water. Most of the plants we grow in our gardens or our homes do not have this ability. Their roots need air, and they can only get it if the soil is allowed to become reasonably dry between waterings. On the other hand, if it were allowed to become bone-dry the roots would be killed by desiccation. So a balance has to be struck. All the same, it is a fact that more plants in pots are killed by too much watering than by too little. You should therefore err on the side of caution, and not offer a plant a drink unless you are satisfied that it really needs one. *If in doubt, don't water*.

In the days when plants in greenhouses and homes were grown in clay pots, it was fairly simple to tell whether water was needed by tapping them on the side with a stick or a small wooden mallet; if a pot gave out a clear ringing note the soil inside was getting dry, but if it made a dull sound the soil was still moist enough. With plastic pots the old method is not much use: plastic pots tend to make a dull sound anyway. Still, it is quite easy to tell the difference by weight. Fill two pots, of the same size, one with wet soil and one with dry. Now lift them and notice how much heavier the one with wet soil is than the other. After doing this a few times you should be able to judge whether a pot needs water or not; if you cannot trust your memory for weight, keep one pot permanently filled with dry soil so that you can always compare the others with it.

There are devices, which can be bought quite cheaply, with probes that are pushed into the soil to show the degree of moisture it contains. One advantage that such a device has is that it can be used outside in the garden, where tapping and weighing are out of the question, but where an apparently dry surface may hide a perfectly adequate degree of moisture an inch or two down.

The fifth principle is that whenever possible watering should be done in the morning or evening, especially in summer, when doing it in the heat of the day may leave drops of water on the plants which can act as tiny lenses, concentrating the sun's rays like burning-glasses and causing scorching. If a plant does droop badly in the sun, and is clearly dying for a drink, be careful not to splash water on the leaves; use the spout of the watering can without a rose on it, and direct the flow of water on to the soil surface. During the winter, watering of greenhouse plants should always be done during the morning; even though not a single drop of water has been splashed on the plants, it is important that the staging should be given as long as possible to dry off before the night.

If garden beds and borders have been properly prepared, with plenty of moisture-holding material (see pages 27–8), watering should rarely if ever be needed. Roots, as we have already seen, should be made to find their own water down below as far as possible. If conditions are right, they should not suffer from undue thirst, except perhaps in a prolonged drought, when of course a ban on watering is likely to be imposed anyway. That is when people lucky enough to have a supply of rainwater score over the rest. A rainwater butt is not too terribly expensive and is quite easy to install; choose one with a lid, otherwise a lot of your precious supply will evaporate away in the hot weather, just when you need it most.

Because of our tremendously increased consumption of water during the last few decades, we shall almost certainly face a serious water shortage in the near future, so it looks as if restrictions on the use of hoses, and perhaps even watering cans, may well get worse, at least during the summer months. So if your beds, borders and/or lawn lack moisture-holding material, and you feel you must water them to prevent them from drying out, you had better do so in the late spring or early summer before restrictions are imposed.

To give the thorough soaking that is necessary, an oscillating sprinkler attached to a hose is ideal – the sort that gives a fan of spray which moves to and fro across the ground. This has the advantage that it waters an oblong patch, which can be easily seen, so that you can then move the sprinkler to an adjoining strip and so avoid overlap. This cannot be prevented with the rotary type of sprinkler, which means too much water is applied to the overlapping bits. The oscillating kind also has the advantage that because the spray is always on the move the ground has plenty of time to absorb the water before the next stroke; it is much better than the lengths of perforated hose that have been on sale for the past few years, because these stay in a fixed position and send out thin jets of water which continually hit the same spot, with the result that where the jet lands becomes completely sodden and the water may run off the surface and be wasted.

Finally, remember that watering the garden should be looked upon as a last resort. Try to improve your soil's water-holding capacity so that watering is rarely if ever needed. And after you have watered, give the surface of the soil a good mulching (see page 38) if you possibly can, to keep the moisture in and stop it evaporating.

THE 'BIG THREE'

We have already seen the vital role that breathing plays in the growth and well-being of plants. But a good supply of fresh air is not only essential to a plant's ability to take in food and make the best use of it, but also to the actual availability of that food. If there is a lack of oxygen in the soil, through waterlogging or some other cause, roots suffer severe deprivation. Excretion, as already explained (page 37), does not only consist of getting rid of the waste products of digestion but also those of respiration, the main elimination product of which is gas. This gas needs to be able to get away easily, not only because it may reach a toxic level if allowed to build up but also because in combination with soil water it may cause high local acidity immediately around the roots, and so prevent them from being able to take in a number of elements, including molybdenum, calcium and the 'big three': nitrogen, potassium and phosphorus.

Of the six major elements, only nitrogen, phosphorus and potassium are normally added to the soil by gardeners. The rest are usually present in sufficient quantities in the earth and in the manures and other substances incorporated with it. So usual is the practice of selling fertilizers to supply one or more of the 'big three' that the standard analysis is expressed in terms of the percentage of nitrogen, phosphorus and potassium contained in them: this is called the NPK Formula.

But plants cannot take in the elements in their pure state, only as certain salts in solution. For instance, though nitrogen is a gas that makes up nearly four-fifths of the air we breathe it is useless as a plant food in that form (though there are minute creatures called nitrogen-fixing bacteria, which live in swellings on the roots of members of the pea and bean family and are able to take nitrogen from the air and turn it into compounds that plants can use). It must be in a form acceptable to the plant's roots. The same applies to the other two elements: in their 'raw' state they would not only be unusable by roots but would severely damage them.

For this reason a fertilizer's value is expressed in terms of how much of each of the three main elements it contains that is actually usable by plants. When you buy a bag of fertilizer you will find that it is labelled with the percentage it contains of nitrogen (N), phosphate (P_2O_5) and potash (K_2O), always in that order. This of course applies only to what are often called 'complete' fertilizers, which contain all three elements; there are also 'compound' fertilizers, containing only two, and 'single' fertilizers, supplying only one. To see why, how, when and in what proportions to apply fertilizers, we must first look at what each of the three main elements does.

The food value of nitrogen

When a young plant is growing strongly it needs a good supply of this element. Nitrogen gives leaves a healthy green colour, and helps increase the size of every part of the plant, which is why it is known as the growth element. In the early stages of a plant's life, when it is opening out after its cramped confinement within the seed, it lives largely on stored food. To ply it with a lot of nitrogenous fertilizer at this stage would be rather like feeding solid food to a newborn baby, with equally damaging effects; until its digestion is strong enough to cope, it is better without additional nitrogen. Indeed, if too much is present in the soil, seeds may fail to germinate at all.

Once vigorous growth has begun, though, nitrogen is what is needed to keep it going. That is why supplies of it should not be allowed to run low, since it is more easily washed out of the soil than the other nutrients. This is particularly true of the nitrate form which, being very soluble, is quick-acting, and so is often given as a kind of tonic. The other forms generally found in nitrogenous fertilizers, ammonium salts and urea, are not usually quite so quickly washed away, at least in soils with a fair proportion of clay.

Fertilizers containing nitrogen come from a variety of sources, and each has its advantages and possible drawbacks. Like all other plant foods, nitrogenous fertilizers may be grouped into two different kinds, according to their source. Those usually called 'organic' come from matter that was once alive; those referred to as 'inorganic', or 'artificial', are purely mineral in origin.

A list of the principal types, both organic and inorganic, is given in the Appendix, which also deals with the amounts needed for good growth.

As far as organic nitrogenous fertilizers are concerned, much depends on what happens to be available locally and at what price. The commonest in general use is probably farmyard manure, which is extremely variable, ranging from excellent stuff worth every penny to complete rubbish. The most consistently reliable is probably hoof and horn meal – rather expensive, but the best for potting composts.

Of inorganic nitrogenous fertilizers, the most widely used by gardeners nowadays is sulphate of ammonia, which is on the whole the most economical too; it is not always the most suitable, though, especially for acid soil, so before making your choice it is best to read the pros and cons on pages 214–16.

SYMPTOMS OF NITROGEN DEFICIENCY. Since nitrogen is the leading growth element, a shortage of it reduces growth. A nitrogen-starved plant is a thin, miserable weakling. Its shoots are few, stiff and upright; side-growths fail to develop so that the plant never becomes bushy. Leaves are small and yellowish, especially the older ones, and they soon turn orange, red or purple, and drop off prematurely. Leaves that have reached these later stages of high (and sometimes rather beautiful) colour cannot be rescued, but if things have not gone too far the plant can be dramatically improved by feeding it with a nitrogenous fertilizer, applied as a liquid feed or a top-dressing, well watered-in if the soil is dry.

SYMPTOMS OF NITROGEN EXCESS. It is all too easy to overfeed plants, especially with nitrogen, so that they become soft and flabby and find it difficult to stand up straight. In such a condition they are very much more likely to fall prey to various diseases, particularly those caused by fungus attack. They are also much less able to face the cold; that is why it is unwise to give nitrogenous fertilizer in late summer or autumn. Unfortunately plants find it difficult to refuse food even when it is bad for them. Even the most grossly overfed baby will, if stuffed with food beyond a certain point, sick some of it up; plants, however, have no such simple way of getting rid of a surfeit, but may be helplessly compelled to take in anything that will go through the surface of the roots whether they need it or not, and even if it poisons them.

There is another highly specific way in which excess of nitrogen can affect a plant. Plants need several different foods in correct proportions to help them grow strong and healthy. Some of the food elements work happily together so that a good supply of one also increases the availability of another: nitrogen and magnesium, for instance, need each other's help to give of their best. A marked excess of nitrogen in nitrate form, however, can turn off the supply of phosphorus to a plant, and so lead to symptoms of phosphate deficiency (see below). So when a plant appears to be suffering from too little phosphorus, think before you rush to administer a stiff dose of phosphate fertilizer: is the trouble really that there is too much nitrate? There is no need to get neurotic about it, because most soils contain enough of everything, and not too much of anything, to suit most plants. Only excessive use of fertilizer can lead to elements fighting each other in this way – at least in normal soil.

The food value of phosphorus

The second of the 'big three' elements, phosphorus, is particularly important for seedlings in their earliest stages; it is the essential infant food, which is why it is often added to seed composts. Newly emerging roots need it for growth and development, and so do the young, unfolding leaves. At the other end of the scale it plays a vital part in bringing about the development of fruit and seeds in the later stages of growth. It helps plants to grow sturdy and independent, assists in bringing about early maturity, and gives added resistance to disease and to cold weather. Because of its 'hardening' effect it guards against the tendency to soft, disease-prone growth brought about by too much nitrogen. In recent times phosphorus has also been shown to be of crucial importance in the process of photosynthesis.

A list of the usually available types of phosphate fertilizers is given on pages 216–18. Of the organics, the most widely used is bone meal, obtainable at all garden stores and commonly recommended for helping good rooting at planting time. Of the inorganics, superphosphate is much the most widely used; it is a highly reliable product and gives excellent results when correctly used.

SYMPTOMS OF PHOSPHATE DEFICIENCY. Since phosphorus is of such vital importance to young plants in the first days of life, lack of it at that stage can have the same sort of effect as undernourishment of a newborn baby, causing feeble growth, poor root development, thin and stunted shoots, and small leaves, often very deep green at first, soon turning a bluish colour and often dull purple later. In severe cases of deficiency older leaves may show scorching round the edges, or suffer from brown spots. The retarding of growth, if not remedied, may lead to a general sickliness, so that the plant is unable to withstand even quite minor variations in weather conditions, such as a sudden rise or fall in air or soil temperature. Not only does phosphorus starvation make for a miserable early youth but it delays the onset of maturity as well. Flower-bud formation is slow and sparse, and the buds may open late, or even fail to develop. Fruiting and seed formation are poor, and any fruit that does develop tends to be patchy in colour, soft, acid and nasty tasting.

There is no rapid cure for phosphate deficiency, since phosphate fertilizers tend to be slow-acting; that is why in the vegetable garden, where deficiency is most likely to occur, such fertilizers are applied in advance, to benefit future crops. However, an obvious deficiency in existing plants stands a fair chance of being remedied by a dressing of superphosphate, lightly hoed in so that it reaches the roots quickly.

SYMPTOMS OF PHOSPHATE EXCESS. Just as too little phosphorus can delay maturity, so too much of it can have the opposite effect. Plants fed with an excessive amount of phosphate have a brief youth, marked by premature hardening and a pallid appearance, followed by unduly hastened maturity and early ripening, often before the fruit is fully developed. Such plants become old before their time. A considerable excess of phosphorus has also been shown to interfere with the uptake of potassium, and of some of the trace elements, particularly iron, copper and zinc. Such severe ill-effects, though, are unlikely to be met with by amateur growers, since the phosphate fertilizers available to them tend, as we have seen, to be slow and gentle in their action.

The food value of potassium

Potassium is of prime importance in giving a plant strength, and increasing its resistance to cold and disease. It helps to produce the sugars and starches needed by plants for their life processes, and its presence in the right quantity is essential to build up and harden the fibrous tissues on which a plant relies to stay firm and avoid flabbiness. It makes leaves a good healthy green, and gives intensity of colour to flowers: many nurseries and garden centres use extra doses of potash fertilizers to brighten up appearances and put customers in the right mood for buying. Both good quality and good colour in fruit are largely dependent on potassium, which is why tomato growers see to it that their plants are given regular helpings of high potash feeds. In short, potash is the 'quality' ingredient in plant food.

The only widely available organic source is wood ash, which can in favourable circumstances be helpful, but if exposed to the weather for any length of time it can become practically useless. Of the inorganics, sulphate of potash is the most widely used, the most consistent and the most reliable. A list of commonly used fertilizers containing potash is given on pages 219–20.

SYMPTOMS OF POTASH DEFICIENCY. The best known and most obvious sign of potash starvation is seen in older leaves, which become pale and unhealthy-looking, and soon develop a typical brown scorching along the edges (marginal leaf burn) and at the end (tip burn). The scorched edges tend to roll under, become wider, and turn crisp and brittle, so that if you rub them between your fingers they crumble to powder. Nothing much can be done with leaves that have reached this state: such advanced symptoms of the deficiency simply show that the trouble was not recognized and dealt with early enough. The first sign of lack of potassium is usually a stunting of growth. Unlike nitrogen deficiency, which causes shoots to be few and spindly, potash deficiency tends to show itself in the production of many short shoots, so that an affected plant looks bushy and squat. In some cases, such as the potato, leaves may become spotty before they develop the characteristic scorching round the edges.

There may be no reduction in flowering at first; in fact one result of potassium deficiency may be that flowers open rather early. However, they tend to drop off quickly, as do any fruit they might set; any fruits that do manage to hang on remain small and immature. If you try to eat a potash-starved apple you will find it not only hard and woody but sweetish in a sickly kind of way, not because it has developed plenty of sugar during ripening but because it has failed to develop the acids that give apples their flavour.

SYMPTOMS OF POTASH EXCESS. Too high a concentration of potash in the soil can do the same sort of damage in the early days of a young plant's life as too much nitrogenous fertilizer. Muriate of potash (potassium chloride) is considerably more dangerous in this respect than sulphate of potash, but even the sulphate must not be overdone, or germination will be reduced and growth suffer. One way to overcome the problem when using straight potash fertilizers is to apply them to the soil in the autumn before digging, so that the potash will be in a milder form when sowing time comes. Or the fertilizer can be applied after the seedlings are well up, and their roots have grown out of the tenderness from which they suffer during the first few days of life.

An excess of potash in the soil can reduce the availability to plants of other elements vital to healthy growth, particularly magnesium. That is why commercial growers of tomatoes, who use heavy dressings of potash fertilizer on their crops to increase the yield of fruit, often have to remedy the magnesium deficiency this causes by giving a feed of Epsom salts (magnesium sulphate).

Some of the minor elements needed for growth are also made unavailable by an excess of potassium, including manganese, copper and zinc. By what is known as an antagonistic reaction, potassium in effect fights these other elements to be taken up by the plant's roots. Potassium wins.

In the plant itself, some nutritionists have described the symptoms of an excess of potassium as a marked check to growth followed by delay in the formation of flowers. It is, however, difficult to give a plant more potassium than it can cope with in ordinary growing conditions; plants seem to be able to take in far more potassium than they actually need without showing any ill effects (a condition known as 'luxury consumption').

DO VEGETARIAN DIETS SUIT YOUNG PLANTS?

The food that a plant takes in through its roots has, as we have seen, been reduced to simple salts dissolved in the soil water, whatever its origin may have been, whether organic or inorganic, animal, vegetable or mineral. Nevertheless, many of the most passionate champions of organic methods of gardening seem to believe that in some mysterious way a vegetarian source of food is superior – hence their advocacy of the compost heap, based on rotting vegetation (with perhaps the addition of farmyard manure, which is only vegetable matter that has passed through animals).

The trouble, as already mentioned, is that the compost heap, however excellent for adding what in terms of human nutrition might be called 'roughage' to the soil, simply cannot be relied upon to supply enough food for vigorous and healthy growth. So the lack must be made up either from animal or from mineral sources. This is where organic enthusiasts who are also vegetarians find themselves in a bit of a fix. They favour only organic fertilizers, but these – hoof and horn meal, dried blood, bone meal, fish meal and so on – involve the slaughter of animals, which goes against their vegetarian principles. Non-animal fertilizers are inorganic, and in most cases subjected to manufacturing processes, and hence 'artificial'.

The problem is really a spurious one. There is no natural law that says that a plant should get its food from organic sources; indeed, even when liberally supplied with such organic material, a plant will take up much of its food from totally inorganic mineral constituents of the soil – clay and rock fragments, extracted from them by weathering, by the action of tiny organisms (with no inhibitions against inorganic foodstuffs) and by secretions from the plant's own roots. A tall forest tree may have roots that go as far down below ground as its trunk rises in the air, and down at those depths there will be little or no organic matter to be found by the roots, which must take nourishment from the underlying rock. The smaller plants we grow in our gardens cannot explore so deeply, and so need their food supplied less far down; and for that purpose inorganic fertilizers are not only suitable but 'natural'.

To sum up the answer to the question with which this section is headed:

1 Generally speaking, a vegetarian diet is not adequate for all the nutritional needs of plants.

2 From the moral point of view, nearly all organic fertilizers involve the slaughter of animals. From the nutritional point of view, they vary widely in composition and food value. From

the economic point of view, they tend to be expensive.

3 Inorganic fertilizers hardly vary at all and you know exactly what you are getting with them. They are clean and do not smell, and they are comparatively cheap.

BALANCED DIETS

Many people find it easier and more convenient to use a 'complete' fertilizer, supplying nitrogen, phosphorus and potassium in one mixture (see page 138). There is a good deal to be said for this: not only does it make life simpler, but there is perhaps less risk of overdoing one element at the expense of others. Many professional growers use these 'convenience foods', reckoning that the slight extra cost is more than repaid by the saving in time and trouble which would be involved in mixing them up oneself.

The most widely used of these ready-mixed fertilizers is probably National Growmore, manufactured to a formula worked out during the Second World War when large numbers of people were taking on allotments, or digging up their lawns and flower-beds to grow vegetables on them, as part of the 'Dig For Victory' campaign. It is a fertilizer containing equal proportions of each of the 'big three' (7% of each), so it is both mild and well balanced; if used at the rate of 3 or 4oz to the square yard (90–125g to the square metre) during the growing season, it will provide just the right stimulus to growth – especially among vegetables, but it is good for beds and borders too – with little or no risk of damage to tender young roots.

You could, if you wished, make up your own National Growmore, or something very like it, by mixing together 5 parts (by weight) of sulphate of ammonia, 5 parts of superphosphate and 2 parts of sulphate of potash; but in the sort of quantity used by amateurs there would be little or no saving in cost, only an unnecessary amount of hard work and a final result probably not as thoroughly mixed as the commercial product.

Many gardeners get excellent results by using only National Growmore as fertilizer, and this certainly makes things easier. However, it is possible to obtain even better results, particularly in the vegetable garden, if you take a little extra trouble and vary the diet according to the time of year. At sowing time in the spring, a fertilizer high in phosphate is ideal; a light sprinkling of plain superphosphate raked into the surface along the rows where seeds are to be sown will often work wonders in improving growth during the first few days. A little later, when the infant plants can take a stronger diet, a fertilizer high in nitrogen will speed things up: say one with 20% N, 10% P_2O_5 and 10% K_2O (usually shortened to 20:10:10), applied at about 1oz to the square yard (30g to the square metre). During the summer another helping may be given to strong-growing crops, either of the same fertilizer or of the one lower in nitrogen, perhaps the 7:7:7 National Growmore already mentioned. As we have seen, you should never use a high nitrogen fertilizer in the late summer or autumn.

A very popular 'complete' fertilizer is the John Innes base, in which the nitrogen, supplied by hoof and horn meal, is not washed away so quickly, because a fair proportion of it is released over a period of time. The John Innes base, a 5.1:6.4:9.7 fertilizer, was developed for pot-plants, and is more fully dealt with on page 78, but many people find its balance of ingredients just right for a last top-dressing to the garden when the days are beginning to shorten, especially among vegetables and fruit, though some use it in flower-beds too.

How should food be given?

When buying fertilizers to use in a dry state on the soil, you will find that you are often offered a choice between granulated and powder forms, particularly with superphosphate and the mixed fertilizers such as National Growmore. For many reasons, it is usually best to buy the granulated form. First, the granules are a uniform size, so it is easy to spread them evenly. Second, they rarely cake together as powder tends to do. Third, with powder the ingredients are not always quite so well mixed, so that results may be a little patchy. Fourth, and perhaps most important, granules are not apt to blow about when you are applying them, so there is little danger of their falling on leaves and scorching them, as can happen with powder when a sudden gust of wind comes along. If you use a mechanical distributor to apply fertilizer, granules have the great advantage that they never clog up the works, as powder is only too apt to do.

Fortunately granular fertilizer is little if any more expensive; indeed, in many cases it is actually cheaper, because it is so popular that it is produced in larger quantities than the powder form, so bringing down the cost; it is also easier to handle, and less wasteful, not only for the gardener but for the manufacturer and retailer too.

Supplementary feeding

So far we have dealt with foods that are applied to the soil in solid form. Should we give supplementary feeds if this seems inadequate in some way?

One must, of course, avoid overfeeding. Fat, flabby plants, like fat, flabby children, are both displeasing to the eye and more prone to ailments of all kinds than are slimmer ones. Starvation is worse still, however, so a watch must be kept to see if supplementary feeds are needed.

Generally speaking, there should be enough nourishment in garden soil, if it is in good condition and fertilizer has been applied where necessary, to see most plants through the growing season – certainly the flowers and trees and shrubs. In some parts of the garden, however, extra feeds with liquid fertilizer can give enormously improved results, particularly with vegetables and fruit.

There are several brands of ready-made fertilizer sold in bottles in concentrated form; when diluted with the amount of water specified on the label, they make a quick-acting liquid feed which is immediately available to be taken up by the roots. When choosing which kind to buy, make sure you get one suitable for the type of crop you want to feed. Though they all contain the 'big three' elements – usually with small quantities of trace elements as well – the proportions of nitrogen, phosphate and potash vary according to the purpose for which the fertilizer is to be used. For leafy crops a high nitrogen content is needed; for fruit a large proportion of potash is the important thing. Tomatoes in full bearing can do with regular drinks, weekly or even twice a week, of special high-potash liquid fertilizer if they are to continue to give heavy crops of top quality fruit.

Vegetables and fruit, however, are not the only things in the garden that have a large amount taken from them during the season and so can benefit from extra feeds to replace what is constantly being lost. A well-kept lawn, regularly mown, has a surprisingly large quantity of grass clippings taken from it during the course of a year, and if it is not fed sooner or later it is bound to become patchy and threadbare; also the finer grasses, which have a shallower rooting system, tend to die out, leaving the ground to be taken over by the coarser species and by vigorous weeds, whose deeper and more pushing roots give them a great advantage in the search for food. Liquid lawn fertilizers are available in con-centrated form, and need to be diluted with water before being applied by a watering can, either through a rose or better still through a dribble-bar attachment (see p. 30), which gives an even band of liquid at the correct rate. When you apply the next band, be careful not to overlap with the previous one, so giving a double dose to the overlapping strip, or to leave a gap that is starved.

Working your way strip by strip across a lawn with a watering can can be an extremely arm-aching job. That is why many people nowadays have switched over to one of the granulated fertilizers. These are applied by means of a wheeled spreader, which is pushed to and fro across the lawn, depositing the fertilizer at a measured rate as it goes. The most modern of these fertilizers contain a coloured material, so that you can see exactly which bit of lawn has been treated. A fertilizer containing a high proportion of nitrogen should be applied in the spring, preferably during showery weather when the ground is moist but the grass itself is dry. Another application or two of the same fertilizer during the summer will keep growth going and replace what is lost by mowing; some very successful gardeners get excellent results rather more cheaply by using only sulphate of ammonia for this summer treatment, at the rate of ½oz to the square yard (15g to the square metre). In the autumn a final feed is needed of a different fertilizer, low in nitrogen, to avoid soft growth vulner-able to harsh weather, but high in phosphate, to build up a good root system and so ensure better growth the following spring. Where weeds are a problem, many people use a combined ferti-lizer and weedkiller for the first or second application during spring or early summer.

Should tonics be given?

A child who is healthy and is getting enough of the right kinds of food has no need of tonics. The same goes for young plants: give them sufficient air and light and an adequate supply of good plain food (but not too much) together with occasional supplementary feeds, and they should grow up to be strong and healthy. The special tonics, in special pictorial packs at special prices, which are offered in bewildering variety at garden shops and centres, are not normally needed. In any case, when a plant is sick or in some way below par it cannot even take in its ordinary food, let alone anything extra.

Not until a plant is well on the road to recovery after an ailment, and is showing definite signs of renewed growth, can a tonic be given. During periods of slow or zero growth, whether through sickness or during an unfavourable season, the roots are not only unable to draw in nourishment properly but may be seriously damaged by contact with plant foods, especially those high in nitrogen. When a plant is on the mend, a suitable tonic may help its convalescence, but be gentle in its use. Make the first application at half strength, and be sure the soil is thoroughly damp beforehand, if necessary by giving a liberal watering. If you have the time and the energy, you can save money by mixing up your own tonic feed according to the formula given on page 81 for pot-plants.

Feeding through the leaves

Professional growers nowadays make considerable use of foliar feeds, which they spray on to the leaves, through which they are absorbed into the plant's system. Such foliar feeds are now available to the amateur, made to a formula which usually includes not only the major elements but the minor ones as well, often in chelated form. Good results can be achieved from them if they are used strictly in accordance with the instructions on the label; err on the safe side by diluting with rather more water than it says. A well-grown plant with a good root system does not normally need feeding through its leaves, however; it can get all the nourishment it wants through its roots.

In exceptional circumstances, when a plant is starved of some essential element, it can be rescued and restored to health by the administration of a foliar feed. A shortage of magnesium, for instance, may be dramatically corrected by one or two sprays with a solution of Epsom salts. Other elements such as boron, molybdenum, manganese, zinc and copper may also be applied as foliar sprays to remedy 'deficiency diseases'. Amateur attempts at diagnosis and cure can do far more harm than good, however, so in cases of deficiency of trace elements, which if given in anything more than infinitesimal amounts can spell death to a plant, expert advice should be sought.

Liquid feeds: ready-made or mix it yourself?

Of the ready prepared brands, those sold as liquid concentrates are somewhat easier to mix with water to the required strength (shake the bottle well first), but are the most expensive, especially if in addition to the major nutrients they contain trace elements as well. Dearest of all are those that include organic substances such as seaweed extract, said by some to be highly beneficial in strengthening growth and warding off disease.

Less expensive are feeds sold as cartons or bags of dry powder or crystals. It may be a little more trouble to mix up a liquid feed from a dry powder than from a bottle, but the saving in cost can be considerable.

Cheapest of all in terms of money, but most expensive in terms of time and effort, is to mix up your own liquid feed from the different ingredients. A very popular formula, tried and tested by commercial growers over more than forty years since it was first developed, is the John Innes Feed (see pages 81–2). It was formulated for the feeding of plants in pots, and that is still its chief use, but it can also be given as a cheap, quick-acting liquid fertilizer in gardens during the spring and summer.

Overfeeding

When giving fertilizers, never use more than the recommended amount. Do not think that twice the dose will produce twice the results; more likely it will cause grave injury – perhaps even death – to the plant.

We have already seen how excess of one element may well 'lock up' other elements, so that they become unavailable to plants, and how an overfed plant is likely to grow soft and flabby, with little resistance to cold, drought, or attacks by pests and diseases. In addition, a high concentration of nutrients – particularly those rich in nitrogen and to a lesser extent potash – immediately near the roots may scorch them and cause them to shrivel, so that they can no longer function properly. The danger is greater with tender infant roots; older ones can cope with a somewhat richer diet, though even they will soon be damaged by excess. Remember that the normal state of affairs is for the sap inside a plant to have a much higher concentration of salts than the soil water outside it. If that situation is reversed, water may be drawn out of the plant instead of into it, so that it becomes dehydrated. That is one reason why fertilizer should always be applied to damp soil; it will then be diluted straight away by the soil water, whereas in dry soil it may remain at a harmfully high concentration even though it has been mixed and applied at the correct strength.

Slow-release fertilizers

The latest additional feeds now available to the amateur (professionals have been using them for some time) are slow-release granules, covered with a special coating which holds in the fertilizer except when conditions of warmth and moisture allow the plants to make use of it. Such feeds are somewhat expensive in their initial cost, and are mostly used for indoor plants at present. In the long run, however, they may prove, outdoors as well as in, both more economical than traditional kinds (because there is no waste) and safer (because they will not scorch the roots).

Can food requirements be measured?

Professional growers of crops have their soil analysed in a laboratory, so that they can see exactly what quantities of the different plant foods are needed. Amateurs can buy soil-testing kits to enable an estimate to be made of the amounts of phosphate and potash present in the soil, so that the quantity needed can be calculated from a chart supplied with the kit. Many kits also include a fluid intended to show whether nitrogen is needed, and if so how much, but this is not very reliable. However, scientists are developing new testing kits which are quicker and easier to use and more reliable than the old ones, and these will soon be on sale to the amateur. When that happens, it will be possible to tell precisely how much of the main plant foods should be given, and so cut down guesswork, starvation and waste.

CHAPTER NINE

Discipline and training

SHOULD CORPORAL PUNISHMENT EVER BE USED?

THERE ARE SOME PEOPLE who believe that a good thrashing is necessary from time to time – or even with some hard cases regularly – to make the young behave properly. Justifying their belief with such sayings as 'Spare the rod and spoil the child', and probably adding 'it never did me any harm', these disciplinarians assert that as a last resort (or in the view of some of them as a first resort) only physical punishment can be relied upon to enforce obedience and discourage unruly conduct.

Though such treatment is more often thought of as being applied to young humans, it has also been inflicted for thousands of years on plants. There are records dating·back to classical antiquity and beyond of regular annual orgies of flagellation in lands bordering the Mediterranean, during which palm trees, olives, figs and other fruit-bearing plants were soundly beaten by members of the local population. The idea behind such rituals seems to have been to propitiate the gods, and so ensure a good harvest. It is unlikely that many people today would claim that sadistic deities needed to be placated in this way. Yet flogging still goes on, not only of children but of plants. A recent enquiry was received by the Forestry Commission's Research Station from a correspondent in Kent asking: 'Why do farmers beat walnut trees in spring and autumn? I have seen it done and I have always wanted to know the reason why.'

A good many people will know the old rhyme:

> A woman, a dog and a walnut tree –
> The more you beat 'em, the better they be

As far as the first two of these objects of assault are concerned, the majority of people nowadays would consider the battering of wives to be both repugnant and wrong, and a growing number of people think the beating of dogs is cruel and counter-productive. So is there anything to be said for the apparently still continuing practice of beating walnut trees? What possible good can it do?

The Forestry Commission referred the question to their Arboricultural Advisory and Information Service, which came up, according to a report of the matter in that respected journal *The Gardener's Chronicle*, with three possible explanations. First, growers of walnut trees for their timber, highly esteemed for the making of fine furniture, may have originated the practice of flogging the trunks in the belief that the injuries so caused to the soft growing tissue just below the bark would result in the formation of burrs in the wood, which would make it more attractive to the eye and therefore more valuable. In fact, the report goes on, the wounds caused by the beating would probably result in the death of the tissue and its infection by decay, so the timber, far from being more valuable, would fetch a lower price.

The second lot of walnut tree floggers cultivated the trees more for their unripe fruits than their timber. They carried out beatings with long poles during the summer, to knock down the young nuts while they were still green and soft enough for pickling. In the course of the thrashing, bits of twig got knocked off the ends of branches, with the result that two or three side-shoots developed fruit during the next season instead of producing one terminal shoot, which would quite likely have yielded only wood. So it could perhaps have been said, in the words of the rhyme, that the beating made the tree 'better', in the sense that it produced more fruit.

The third and perhaps the most likely explanation is the belief that harsh treatment can, by restricting growth, bring about earlier and more prolific fruiting. It is widely accepted – and sometimes even true – that a plant suffering from great stress, whether from injury or some other cause such as drought, will somehow sense that its last days are upon it and respond by bearing lots of fruit, even though it is too young to do so normally, in an attempt to produce offspring before it dies. This belief is responsible for the practice by some fruit-growers of deliberately mutilating or withholding water from immature trees, in order to force them into bearing at an early age; such methods are used by Italian olive-growers to speed up cropping. And so walnut trees have for centuries been thrashed, not only with sticks but with whips and chains – and, what is more, the practice still persists in some places.

A year or two ago, the *Gardener's Chronicle* report reminds us, an enthusiastic walnut-whacker was shown on television mercilessly flogging his tree with a chain. When he was asked why he did it, he claimed that if he neglected to beat the tree for a couple of years the crops diminished and the nuts tended to drop off before they were ripe. He added that the tree needed a good hiding every two or three years 'to wake it up and remind it that it was there to produce nuts'.

Before those who find beating repugnant become too disheartened by this apparent evidence that flogging pays, it is a relief to find that the report concludes by pointing out that much better results can be obtained by gentler and more intelligent methods. To quote from the final words: 'Before walnut tree owners rush into their gardens armed with sticks, flails, chains and bull whips, it is suggested that in these days of scientific and technological advances, a less damaging and probably more successful approach would be to ensure that your walnut trees are healthy, not too vigorous as a result of excess water and nutrients, and properly pruned. In this way they are more likely to produce fruit naturally and regularly, and to continue for many years without being beaten to death.'

In short, though harsh and violent treatment may seem to pay off in the short term, the truth seems to be that a combination of healthy conditions, good food (but not too much of it), kindness and understanding, together with enough patience and tolerance to let them develop at their own pace, will produce much better and more lasting results than the short sharp shock.

CUTTING BACK TREES

Since punishment seems to be of little or no use, should we discipline our plants at all? Why not leave them alone to behave as they wish? The answer is twofold. First, most of the plants we grow in our gardens, and all of those we grow in our homes and greenhouses, are not in their native environment; they lead a sheltered life, protected from the various things that would naturally keep them under control, such as the animals which in the wild would be nibbling their shoots and browsing on their foliage. So we have to mow our lawns for the lack of grazing cattle to do the job for us; and we substitute shears and scissors for the beaks of the grouse which keep the heather in trim on the moors.

Second, though we need to know as much as possible about the nature of our charges, whether plants or children, so that we can work *with* that nature rather than *against* it, there comes a point when natural tendencies need to be curbed in the interest of harmony. Some individuals in any community, human or vegetable, are pushing and assertive, and unless they are checked they will soon overwhelm the less forceful ones. Even then, however, the checking should wherever possible take the form of persuasion rather than of trying to cut the over-assertive plant down to size – an action, as we shall see, likely to cause resentment and to lead to even more aggressive behaviour later on.

Since the problem is really one of too much exuberance, it is usually possible to avoid the difficulty, or at any rate to lessen it, by choosing less exuberant plants.

The thing to be avoided at all costs is a plant that will have to be kept constantly in check, in a way that violates its nature, in order to fit into the restricted conditions which are all you can give it.

When buying trees, find out how tall they will be when full-grown and how wide their branches will spread. Then you will be able to visualize how they will eventually look in relation to the house, the rest of the garden and each other. To assist your imagination and to avoid mistakes, draw a plan of your garden to scale on graph paper, mark the positions of the trees you intend to plant, and draw a circle round each showing the spread its branches will reach when full-grown. By rubbing out and re-arranging as necessary, make sure these circles do not overlap each other or touch the house. It is much easier to correct errors on paper than to try to do so later on in the garden itself.

PRUNING

A great deal of physical assault, in the form of quite unnecessary lopping and chopping, still goes on even when there is no excuse on grounds of lack of space. In most cases, this is probably because people have heard or read somewhere that they ought to be doing something called pruning. Having only the vaguest idea what this means, they go in for an orgy of aimless cutting, in the hope that they are doing the right thing.

There would be less senseless mutilation if people would obey the simple rule never to prune at all unless they can give a very good reason for doing so. The worst reason of all is an attempt to restrict a naturally robust and outgoing personality. The attempt is in any case almost certain to backfire. Understanding is what is needed, and that understanding might best begin with the realization that there is a natural balance in development, an inbuilt self-control, which is governed by the restraining influence of inhibition; ignorant and insensitive treatment may succeed in removing the inhibition and so cause that self-control to be lost.

The natural balance that shapes the character of a tree or shrub may be traced back to its roots. There is always in any normal, healthy plant an inbuilt disposition for the amount of root growth and the amount of top growth to balance each other. If therefore you cut top growth back hard but leave the roots intact, the plant will react by trying to restore the balance as quickly as it can. And the quickest way is to produce several new shoots for each one that was removed; by this means there will soon be sufficient leaf surface again to draw up and breathe out the quantity of water that that amount of root extracts from the soil. (This need for balance is why, at the other extreme, newly taken cuttings often have a large amount of leaf clipped off by experienced propagators, to prevent too much water being exhaled before roots have formed.)

If a tree or shrub is allowed to develop normally, it will produce the required amount of leaf on a limited number of shoots, well placed, well spaced and pleasing to the eye. The natural restraint shown by such plants in limiting the number of shoots is caused by a hormone produced at the tip of each shoot, the effect of which is to inhibit the growth of buds lower down. If you cut off the end of the shoot, you remove this natural inhibition, and there is nothing to stop the buds bursting into growth to restore the root/shoot balance. So a thicket of new shoots forms, spoiling the plant's natural beauty. That is all very well if you want to impose an artificial shape, in the form of a hedge or a piece of topiary work, because the continual clipping encourages the dense growth that is needed.

In a vast number of cases, however, such treatment would be

gravely wrong. Not only would the proliferation of shoots rob the plant of its grace and charm, but overcrowding of stems may lead to disease. Plenty of light and air is essential to most plants for healthy growth.

Before you cut anything, then, remember that generally speaking *pruning does not reduce growth but increases it*. And in doing so it prolongs immaturity. Since that is the immediate effect of cutting back plants, perhaps we should deal with it as the first of several reasons for doing so.

Pruning to prevent or delay growing up

Plants, as explained in chapter 7, go through various changes as they approach sexual maturity. Many gardeners try to prevent or delay adulthood in some plants in order to retain appealing juvenile habits and appearance.

One of the most obvious examples of this is the growing interest in the Japanese art of Bonsai, by which trees in pots are artificially kept dwarf. Though a few kinds with very small berries may be allowed to bear a limited number of flowers and fruit, in most cases all such attempts at development are deliberately suppressed. The dwarfing process is a continuous and elaborate one, involving not only repeated cutting and pinching of shoots but also regular pruning of roots, to preserve the balance between growth above and below the soil level. To force growth into the desired shape, various devices are employed, such as twisted wires, weights, clamps and splints – the binding of infant girls' feet, to restrict their growth to a size considered attractive, was practised for centuries in the same part of the world that gave us Bonsai. Some of the most treasured products of the art are ancient dwarfs several centuries old and still living their restricted lives. They are admired with reverential awe by addicts at shows, where, in the somewhat poignant words of an authoritative handbook* giving detailed guidance on the subject, top marks go to those specimens which most successfully hide the scars inflicted by the treatment they have received. It should be added that many trees will not put up with such treatment; they are, to quote the handbook, 'unsuitable or uncontrollable', and readers are

* *Bonsai*, Wisley handbook 40 (Royal Horticultural Society, 1981).

cautioned not to attempt to dwarf 'any tree which has too much will of its own'.

Another severe form of pruning is practised with the object of producing new young shoots each year which are cut right down after their first season, to be replaced the following year by a fresh crop of juvenile shoots. The result is that the stems are never more than one year old and the plant never develops a natural shape. This very drastic treatment is reserved for those species whose beauty lies in the coloured bark of their young shoots. One spectacular example is the white-stemmed bramble, *Rubus cockburnianus*, whose stems glint in the winter sunshine as if they had been painted with a thick coating of whitewash; it has some close relatives of similar habit and beauty. These decorative brambles, like their relation the raspberry, produce new shoots as suckers from the base and are pruned in the same way, by cutting all previous growth right down to ground level in the spring.

Other kinds with coloured bark on the young stems include many species and varieties of willow, with shoots ranging in colour from white bloom over purple through golden to orange, and the dogwoods, *Cornus alba* and *C. stolonifera*, which have varieties whose stems are coloured bright crimson, purplish black, yellow and olive-green. Since these willows and dogwoods would if left unpruned develop into trees or shrubs, pruning for the production of young shoots consists of annually cutting main stems back to two or three buds above ground level, in early spring. If, because of the contour of the ground or because there is something in the foreground which obscures the view, you want to be able to see the coloured stems in a higher position, you can pollard the willow or dogwood: that is, you can allow a main trunk to develop to the height you wish, and then cut the young stems sprouting from the top of that trunk back to two or three buds each spring.

Pruning to assist development

Apart from pruning to stave off adulthood, as just described, most pruning is designed to help the plant to develop so that it produces its flowers when it has reached a size and shape that will show them off to full advantage. This will sometimes mean removing the tip of a shoot to induce other shoots to grow out from buds lower down the stem, and so postpone flowering for a while, until there are plenty of fresh flower-buds formed on the new shoots, which will open at the same time and give a mass display.

This is, of course, what is habitually done to annuals, and to some perennials, when their tips are nipped off at planting time to make them bush out and develop a well-rounded shape before they flower. Because the growth is soft and the nipping out is done between finger and thumb instead of with knife or secateurs, the operation is called 'pinching out', but it is of course a form of pruning.

The term pruning is, however, usually applied to the cutting of woody or semi-woody growths by the use of some instrument designed for the purpose. At its simplest it merely consists of the removal of unwanted material. The most obvious example is what is known as 'dead-heading', the process of cutting off flowers when they begin to fade. There are basically two reasons for this operation. The first is that faded flowers are simply unattractive to look at. The second is to avoid unwanted pregnancy and produce more flowers. Flowers are merely devices of nature to produce fruit and seeds, and (unless of course you want the fruit to mature) you need to frustrate the process as early as possible, before the production of offspring takes up the plant's energy and resources. If the first attempt to produce offspring is prevented, the plant will try again with another lot of flowers. But only those plants that have the ability to produce more than one crop of flowers will respond – which for practical purposes means herbaceous plants of many kinds, plus a few things like the modern rose hybrids, which respond to cutting by producing new flowering shoots.

Most trees and shrubs do not flower more than once during the season. The majority form their blossom-buds on mature wood that is two years old or more. Since any shoots younger than that have not yet reached flowering age, pruning should be kept to a minimum, otherwise you will get a thicket of young growth and no blossoms. It is failure to recognize this simple fact that causes so much frustration, both to the pruner and to the pruned.

Anyone who has spent time answering gardeners' questions will have received the sort of letter that starts, 'I never get a good crop of apples, although I prune my tree every year.' The only possible reply is, 'You never get a good crop of apples probably *because* you prune your tree every year.' Such little cutting as needs to be done to species that flower on mature wood should be confined to the removal of dead, diseased or damaged growth, and the cutting out of overcrowded shoots, particularly any growing inwards towards the middle. That will make the plant both more attractive to look at and healthier, because it will let in light and air. Occasionally it may be necessary to remove a branch that is awkwardly placed so that it spoils the shape of the plant, or to take out a coarse shoot that is growing much faster than the rest and so ruining the balance – or even threatening to take over completely by robbing the other growths of their fair share of sap. Such shoots are best cut right out at the base.

Shrubs which flower on young shoots

Some shrubs produce their flowers on young shoots. Such shrubs fall into two types. The first flower on the previous year's wood; since no wood older than that will ever flower again, these shrubs tend to become leggy, because the new growth that will bear next year's blooms appears at the end of bare branches no longer capable of flowering. To make matters worse, in the following year that new growth will in its turn have become old and bare, so a further crop of new shoots will have to be produced from the end of it to bear next year's flowers. Pruning is easy if you keep in mind that with this type of shrub *the stems are already too old by the age of two*. What you should do, therefore, is to cut them right back as soon as they have finished flowering to a basal bud or shoot. In this way you will keep up the supply of young shoots to flower next year, and keep down the amount of useless old wood past flower-bearing age. The shrub will then stay compact, with flowers at eye-level instead of at the ends of long, ungainly stems. Some of the shrubs suitable for this treatment are *Buddleja alternifolia*, *Spiraea arguta* ('Bridal Wreath') and all the species and varieties of *Deutzia*, *Forsythia*, *Kerria*, *Philadelphus*, *Ribes* and *Weigela*.

Some of the shrub roses which produce their best flowers on the previous season's wood are also pruned in this way. At one time many gardeners cut them back as severely as they did hybrid teas (dealt with in the next section), but in our more permissive age they are usually given gentler treatment, the aim being to leave enough mature framework to make a shapely and attractive bush even when not in flower. Rambler roses are also best pruned immediately after flowering; ideally they should have enough strong new shoots growing from the base to replace the old stems, which should be cut right down to ground level, but if there are not enough new growths to cover the space fully, one or two of the old stems may be left for another year, their side-shoots which have just finished flowering being cut back to two or three buds.

The second type of shrub that calls for hard pruning is the kind that flowers in late summer or autumn on young shoots produced during the same year. From the start of growth in the spring, these have at most only seven or eight months to become mature enough to flower, since after that all further growth stops for the winter. By the following spring, when growth starts again, those shoots will be well past flower-bearing age. Pruning must therefore be governed by the fact that with shrubs of this type *shoots are already too old at the age of one year*. Last year's shoots should be cut right back to one or two buds as soon as growth starts in early spring, so as to give the new shoots as long as possible to develop before they are called upon to bear flowers.

Some of the most popular shrubs suitable for this treatment are that favourite of the butterflies, *Buddleja davidii*, with its many splendid varieties bearing flowers of purple, violet, lilac, cream and white, and many others including *Caryopteris*, *Ceanothus* of the deciduous type, *Ceratostigma*, *Fuchsia*, *Passiflora* and late-flowering kinds of *Spiraea*, such as *S. japonica* and *S. douglasii*.

Since the most widely grown of all roses, the hybrid teas and floribundas, also flower on the current season's growth, they too benefit from hard pruning each year, to produce top quality blooms, to stop the bushes from becoming leggy and top-heavy, and to keep up a supply of healthy, thrusting new shoots. There is, however, a certain amount of argument among rose experts over the question of what is the best time to perform the operation. Some say it should be done in the dead of winter when the plants are dormant (and incidentally when there is little else to do), because at that time they will not have wasted any of their energy in starting to make growth which will then be cut away. Others say that winter pruning is rash and that the operation is best left till mid-spring, when the swelling buds on the stems show that growth is starting. Most people, particularly in cold districts where very severe frosts are likely, take the second view. In any case, it is a wise precaution in exposed situations to do some preliminary pruning in the autumn by cutting off the top third or so of all tall growths to lessen the danger from high winds, which can inflict serious damage if they are allowed to rock top-heavy bushes.

Deal most severely with the weak

The guiding principle where the pruning of shrubs is concerned is simply this: *always treat the weakest with the greatest severity.* Every pruning operation should start with the cutting out completely of all dead, dying, damaged or diseased wood. It is important that you should always cut back to healthy growth. If there is a brown stain in the wood, it means that there is an infection at that point, so you must cut back still further, again and again if necessary, to clean wood with no sign of staining; only then can you be sure that you have done everything possible to get rid of a source of further infection. Having removed all dead, damaged and diseased wood, you should then remove any feeble, twiggy and sickly-looking growths, together with any causing overcrowding. Then comes the question of how much to cut back the shoots that are left, and the answer is to deal most severely with the least robust and most leniently with the strongest. A stout and vigorous shoot, for instance, may be left intact except perhaps for the removal of the unripe tip, while at the other end of the scale the thinnest and shortest shoot may be cut back to two or three buds. The reason for what might seem like a reversal of normal human feelings about when to be tough and when to be tender is the fact that, as already explained, generally speaking pruning stimulates growth: the strong shoot does not need stimulus but the weak shoot does.

Treatment of cuts and bruises

All cuts and open wounds are potentially dangerous sources of infection, so everything possible should be done to assist rapid healing so as to keep out disease germs. The most important thing, before any cutting is done, is to make sure that all pruning instruments are sharp and bright, so that they never cause bruising or leave jagged edges. Some experts still use a knife, but nowadays most amateurs, and an increasing number of professionals, use secateurs, preferably with a slicing action, which give excellent results if they are well looked after and never used for cutting wood too thick for them, which may strain them and put the blades out of alignment.

Besides sharp tools, the best way to ensure rapid healing is to remember never to leave any surplus wood behind after the operation which will prevent the growth of a covering of healing tissue. When removing a shoot completely, be sure to cut it off flush, leaving no 'snag', which apart from preventing the cut from healing over is bound to die back and may introduce disease in the process. This is particularly important if you ever have to remove a branch of some age and thickness that needs to be sawn off. Never leave a 'hat-peg'. First saw the underside of the unwanted branch upwards for an inch (2.5 cm) or two where it joins the trunk, so as to ensure that it does not come crashing down, tearing a strip of bark with it. Then saw downwards at the junction of branch and trunk, making the cut absolutely flush. The rough surface of the wound left by the saw-teeth invites disease and decay, so it should be pared smooth with a sharp knife. As an additional precaution, it is good hygienic practice to paint over the surface to exclude disease spores. There are special paints on sale for the purpose containing fungicides, but ordinary exterior-grade paint left over from house decorating will do; if the colour looks incongruous, it will soon be covered with healing tissue.

The same principle applies also to the cutting back of shoots to produce new growth. Always make the cut just above a bud, so that no useless wood is left to die back and cause trouble. A correct cut starts level with the bud on the opposite side of the shoot and slopes upwards slightly, so that it finishes just above the bud without damaging it. Do not make the slope too steep, or you will not only elongate the cut, leaving an unnecessarily large wound exposed, but risk reducing the food supply to the bud and so starving it out and causing it to die; the bud below it will then become the growing point, and you will have left above it just the useless snag you wanted to avoid.

Be consistent in your treatment

A tree or shrub left to its own devices will, if properly fed and healthy, develop its own character and establish its own life-style. That is all very well so long as you are happy with its character and its life-style does not interfere with others. What causes trouble is when it has been allowed to go its own way, maybe for years, and then an attempt is made to force it to change its ways, perhaps because it no longer fits in with the other inhabitants of the garden or with your own changed notions of training, or because its untidy ways have become too much for you, or simply to make room for a new arrival in the garden. Drastic measures may then have to be taken, such as the cutting back of mature wood which has long enjoyed an interference-free existence. The shock may kill the plant, or (and some may consider this worse) it may live on, unbalanced, misshapen and permanently scarred.

The lesson is that such a state of affairs should never be allowed to occur if it can possibly be avoided. Attend to pruning as and when it is needed; do not keep putting it off till drastic action is required. Young wood is easier to cut, more amenable to training and quicker to heal than older wood that has become set in its ways.

SUPPORT OR INDEPENDENCE?

A great many plants are perfectly capable of supporting themselves without any outside aid, from annuals and the sturdier herbaceous perennials to trees and shrubs, whose woody framework has been developed for that very purpose. Many other plants are not so self-reliant. These include several tall-growing herbaceous garden hybrids such as the stately modern delphiniums with their long spires of brilliant flowers; though the parent species from which the breeders have developed them are, like most natural species, of moderate height and able to stand up by themselves, their unnaturally lofty offspring cannot manage without being propped up.

It is not only hybrid garden perennials that need support. There are many natural climbers and scramblers which in their native environment cling to trees, shrubs, rocks or anything else available by means of thorns, spines and tendrils, or twine themselves by their stems or their leaf-stalks round any branch or twig they can find. These are the kinds that make admirable subjects for covering arches, pergolas or even dead trees or bushes, and for clothing the walls of a house. The easiest are those known as self-clingers, which attach themselves with aerial roots, like the ivy, or with sucker pads, like the Virginia creepers; they need no other support than the wall itself. Others need something they can twine round or be tied to, such as trellis or a network of wires held an inch (2.5 cm) or so out from the wall by being threaded through vine-eyes made of galvanized steel and either hammered or screwed into the wall.

In addition to those plants that need support all their lives, there are others that need it during their first few years. A tree growing in the spot where it germinated will have anchored itself firmly into the soil, from the time its first rootlet sprouted, with a complex and ever-widening root system which holds it tenaciously in place against fierce winds. A tree transplanted from a nursery may take several seasons to send out a strong enough root system to make it self-supporting, and it should therefore be securely staked at the time of planting.

It is totally misguided to deny a plant support just when it needs it most, because of some mistaken notion that making it stand up for itself will teach it independence. So make a point of giving support to any plant that needs it as early as possible. In the herbaceous border those plants that are going to need support should be staked when the new growth starts in spring. For most subjects a pea-stick or two stuck into the ground so that the plant grows up through them should be enough; for very tall plants which produce their flowers on long single spikes it may be better to use stout bamboo canes, to which the growths are tied as they develop. In either case make sure that the stakes are shorter than the height the plant will reach; they will then be invisible by the time it flowers.

Climbers and wall shrubs should have their new growths trained into place on their supports as they develop. In the vegetable garden stakes for peas and beans should be put in when the seeds are sown. The earlier support is given the less likelihood there is that the vulnerable young plants will flop to the ground and perhaps develop kinks from which they may not recover. In the words of the Book of Proverbs (but substituting 'plant' for 'child'): 'Train up a child in the way he should go: and when he is old, he will not depart from it.'

Weaning

There are now special units, called weaner units, in commercial nurseries and some amateur greenhouses where mist propagation is used for raising plants (see page 67). Their function is to accustom the young cuttings, when they are well rooted, to more normal life after the very special treatment they have received in their early days. It has been found that such plants can suffer a severe shock if suddenly deprived of what they have been used to: a very fine spray of water, at regular and fairly frequent intervals. The object of the weaner unit, to quote from a sales brochure put out by a leading supplier of mist propagation equipment, is that by step-by-step reduction in the frequency of misting 'cuttings can be gradually weaned away from the full mist regime, thereby avoiding any checks which might otherwise arise through the sudden withdrawal of atmospheric moisture when planting out'. It is interesting, and somehow rather reassuring, to learn that even cloned plants, raised in artificial and scientifically controlled conditions, cannot have their habits abruptly altered without suffering damaging consequences. If you are thinking of installing mist propagation it is highly advisable to go to the further expense of having a weaner unit; otherwise you may discover the hard way, through high levels of infant mortality among your mist-raised plants, that you must not change the routine of the young too suddenly.

A more usual form of what might be termed weaning is the process known as 'hardening off'. This is a method of gradually accustoming a young plant to lower temperatures. Many half-hardy plants are raised from seed sown in heat under glass while it is still too cold outside, and later planted out in the open when the weather is warmer. Once again if the change from indoors to outdoors were too sudden, the health, and maybe the life, of the plant would be at risk. Instead of being planted straight from a warm greenhouse into the open ground, the tender young seedling is put for a transition period into a frame, closed at first during cold weather and gradually opened more and more as the days become longer and warmer. After a week or two of this gradual acclimatization the plant should be hardened sufficiently to be planted outside with a fair chance of surviving our somewhat uncertain summers.

CHAPTER TEN

Desirable and undesirable companions

AS ALL PARENTS KNOW, it is practically impossible to choose the company your children keep. You face much the same problems in bringing up plants – except that they do not choose their companions: the companions choose them.

Companions, good and bad, come in two kinds: animal and vegetable. We will deal with the animal ones first. Many of them can cause a great deal of damage, especially in the early stages of a plant's life, when it is at its most vulnerable. For instance, if a newly emerged seedling has its first pair of leaves bitten off at the stem, it will have little or no chance of recovery, whereas later in its life it may have quite a large part of its leaf area nibbled away and still be able to survive and even to flourish.

Apart from the odd mammal such as a rabbit or a mouse, which can wreak havoc, or a cat scratching up the seed-bed, obviously the creatures that do the most damage to plants are those which live on a vegetable diet. Most of these vegetarian pests are various kinds of insects, of which there are a terrifying number.

FRIENDLY ANIMALS

Before dealing with undesirable companions, though, let us look at some of the desirable ones, the friends of plants and of those who grow them. There are plenty of these helpful creatures; indeed, the number of plant friends must be at least as great as that of plant enemies, otherwise the vegetable kingdom would have been destroyed long ago. In a wider sense, everything lives on plants in the long run, because only plants have the ability to build themselves up by using the energy of sunlight. Animals, lacking this ability, are all parasitic on plants in the end, but from the gardener's point of view they can be divided into good types and bad types, according to their eating habits. The bad ones live on plants, while the good ones live on the pests that live on plants. It is, of course, the good types that we want to encourage. In order to do so, we must first be able to recognize and understand them.

If it moves, leave it alone. With few exceptions, friends are quick and enemies are slow. The reason is quite simple. Since plants cannot move about, the pests that feed on them do not have to hurry to catch them; vegetarians can take their meals at leisure. Indeed, some of the most pernicious pests, such as scale insects, which feed themselves by piercing a plant's skin and sucking out its vital juices, may remain attached to the same spot most of their lives, gorging themselves on one continuous liquid meal.

The gardener's friends, on the other hand, are carnivorous, and like all hunters they have to be able to move fast, so that they can pounce on their prey before it has time to escape.

Feathered friends

Leave birds alone. Most of the time they do very little harm and a vast amount of good. A friendly robin, for instance, which follows you round as you dig and hoe and weed, eats large quantities of insects, grubs and other pests; it probably thinks you crazy to be uncovering so many delicacies and not eating them yourself. Its near relative the thrush is a highly efficient killer of snails, which it bashes against a stone to get at the meat inside. Many small birds consume large quantities of greenflies on the stems of plants, without damaging the plants themselves.

Sometimes birds can be pests, pecking up newly sown seeds, or shredding flowers with their sharp beaks. Some birds, particularly the bullfinch, do a great deal of damage to fruit. (For suggestions on how to prevent this kind of damage see page 188.) In spite of these few acts of vandalism, birds are useful creatures: without them there would be a massive increase in the number of pests.

Frogs and toads

If you are lucky enough to have these in your garden, count your blessings. Both frogs and toads have an enormous appetite for insects, grubs, slugs, snails, woodlice, beetles, caterpillars, ants and other such pests.

A toad in a greenhouse can work wonders in keeping the place free from pests. Do not attempt to pick it up; its warty skin contains glands that secrete an irritant poison, with which it wards off attacks by such creatures as weasels, causing irritation of the mouth, slowing of the heart, and paralysis of the muscles.

Hedgehogs

A hedgehog is another good friend to have in the garden. It devours a mixed diet of slugs, worms, insects, grubs and beetles, and likes a little soft (and preferably decaying) vegetable matter with its meat. It is active at night, and if you go out in the garden and stand very still you will often hear its snorts and grunts. Hedgehogs can be encouraged to become regular visitors if you put out a saucer of bread and milk for them in the evening – plus any odd scraps of meat you may have left over. This is specially welcome in the autumn, when they like to stuff themselves with food, which is turned into masses of fat to help them survive through the winter. Do not continually go out when darkness falls, armed with a torch and perhaps accompanied by noisy, excited children, to see if any hedgehogs are taking your offered meal: they are shy creatures, and can easily be scared away. You must be content to discover next morning that the food has disappeared.

Shrews

Unlike mice, which can do a great deal of damage by devouring newly sown seeds and nibbling plants, shrews are carnivorous. They have a prodigious appetite and can in one day eat their own weight in beetles, snails, slugs, grubs and worms, which they search out with their long, sensitive snouts. They need to eat almost incessantly: they will starve to death quicker than any other small mammal.

A helpful slug

Though most slugs are among the gardener's bitterest enemies, there is actually one kind that is among the gardener's best friends. It is called the shield-shelled slug (known scientifically as *Testacella haliotidea*), and unlike other slugs, which as gardeners

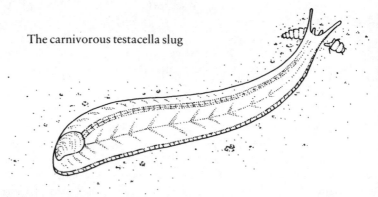

The carnivorous testacella slug

know to their cost are strict vegetarians, it is a meat-eater. It hides in the ground during the day and comes out at night to feed on a rich, high-protein diet of worms, grubs, millipedes, and, best of all, ordinary slugs, which it relishes greatly. The testacella slug can be easily recognized by the small, ear-shaped shell it carries on its behind. This shell is much too small to house it; in fact it is not a home at all but probably a shield to protect the creature's backside. If you find any shield-shelled slugs in the garden, leave them in peace.

Ladybirds and crocodiles

There are several different kinds of ladybirds, some yellow and some red, and spotted in various patterns. The commonest in the British Isles is the one with bright red wing cases marked with black spots. Their young are commonly called 'crocodiles', because they resemble them on a small scale. They are extremely valuable allies of the gardener; they greedily devour those most widespread of all plant pests, the aphids (greenfly, blackfly and their host of nasty relatives). Unfortunately after a cold winter ladybirds often do not appear in sufficient numbers until aphid populations have built up to epidemic proportions, but once the young hatch out in force they can make short work of even the heaviest infestation; indeed, when there are no aphids left it is not unknown for the crocodiles to turn cannibal and start eating each other.

Beetles

There are something like a quarter of a million different species of beetle in the world, over 3,000 of them in the British Isles alone. Many of them are serious plant pests, so much so that there is a widespread belief that the only good beetle is a dead beetle. That is not so at all; some of the gardener's best friends are beetles. The problem is to be able to distinguish friends from foes. Appearance is not enough. Some of the fiercest-looking are in fact the mildest of vegetarians: the armour-plated stag beetle, with notched antlers and threatening jaws, which looks capable of killing anything, is only just able to pierce the skin of a plant, and lives on sap.

Among beetles that the gardener can count as friends are the carabids, much less formidable-looking but some of the most ferocious killers in the garden. A typical one, the violet ground-beetle, which hides in the soil or under a stone during the day, becomes at night a ruthless and greedy destroyer of any living thing it can get the better of: other beetles, insects of all kinds, slugs, snails, or anything else weaker or less nimble than itself. And when mating is over, the female eats the male.

Other harmless-looking but useful creatures are the pretty tiger beetles, no more than an inch (2.5 cm) long and clad in armour like polished metal, glinting green and blue. They devour any insects or other small creatures they can catch, and when hunting can run and fly at great speed. They lay their eggs in the earth, and the grubs when they hatch out wriggle down, tail first, just below the surface. When they want a meal they stick their heads up just far enough to be able to grab any passing small creature with their pincer-like jaws and drag it down into the ground.

Perhaps the most easily identified of carnivorous beetles is the devil's coach horse. It is black all over, holds its belly up in the air when running, and when threatened lifts up its head and its tail in a menacing way and gives out a most disgusting smell from two stink glands at its rear end. Few pests stand a chance of escaping from its powerful jaws. It is not at all choosy in its diet: if there is no live prey about, it is quite content to chew up dead bodies, however smelly and decomposed they may be. In fact it is thoroughly at home among nasty smells, since when not active it likes to spend its time hidden in dung. When the devil's coach horse curls its spiky rear end forward over its back it looks rather like a scorpion, but it carries no sting in the tail. Do not pick it up though: it can give you quite a painful bite.

Centipedes

The species of centipede found in our gardens are wholly beneficial, yet millions of them are destroyed by gardeners in the mistaken belief that they are pests. The trouble is that people confuse them with the harmful millipedes, which do an enormous amount of damage by gnawing their way into roots and tubers.

Centipede: a plant friend

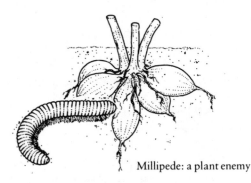

Millipede: a plant enemy

Yet there is no reason at all to confuse them. Millipedes, being vegetarian, move sluggishly; along most of their body they have two pairs of short, hair-like legs to each segment; they are usually slate-coloured, and they curl themselves into a flat spiral when alarmed. Centipedes, on the other hand, rush about in search of their insect prey. They have only one pair of legs to each body segment and are reddish brown in colour, shining like well polished leather. So if you see one scuttling about in the soil, leave it unmolested to go about its work of pest destruction.

Lacewings

Adult lacewings are those very beautiful creatures, with two pairs of greenish transparent wings marked with an intricate tracery of veins, which can be seen flitting about the garden on sunny days. Despite their delicate looks they are ruthless hunters, with prominent compound eyes to enable them to spot likely prey. They have jaws built for chewing, and mouth-parts with which they seize the prey and suck out its juices; they then discard the empty skin of the aphid and move on to the next victim. Sometimes they entangle the remains of their victims among the bristles with which their bodies are covered, and wear them like a strange outer garment. Whether they do so to hide themselves from enemies, to make themselves look bigger and more formidable, or simply to paralyse their victims with fear, we do not know for certain.

The eggs of the lacewing also look extremely odd. Instead of laying them direct on the leaves or stems of plants, the female first touches the surface with her abdomen, from which she deposits a drop of liquid; she then raises herself up so as to draw out this liquid, which instantly dries in contact with the air to form a thread, and on the end of this she fixes her egg. She continues in this way till her supply is exhausted, leaving a miniature thicket of eggs on stalks. The reason for this strange performance is not fully known, but it is thought that being raised on stalks gives the eggs some protection from ants and other roving creatures. Whatever the explanation, this unusual method of laying makes them instantly recognizable. So if you discover eggs on stalks, do not squash them but let them hatch out into some of the most eager and effective aphid-destroyers in the world.

Hoverflies

There are several different species of these useful insects, all with the ability to hover in the air apparently motionless, their wings going so fast that the movement can hardly be seen; from time to time they make sudden darts and then stay motionless again.

Most species are striped, so that they look rather like small wasps. Their eggs hatch out into flattish, semi-translucent grubs somewhat resembling miniature slugs. Their method of consuming aphids is highly efficient, and fascinating to watch if you are not too squeamish. They seize the aphid, lift it into the air, puncture its skin, suck out its insides, and then spit out the empty husk. A single hoverfly grub, crawling along the stem of an infested plant, is capable of disembowelling hundreds of aphids an hour.

Useful parasites

On the whole, parasites get very bad publicity. They are accused of living off others and doing nothing for their living. Yet without parasites to keep their numbers in check, plant pests would be a much worse menace than they are.

Typical of helpful parasites are the ichneumon flies, members of the largest order of British insects known as the Hymenoptera, which also includes ants, bees and wasps. One particularly useful species, *Apechthis rufata*, a black, ½-inch (1 cm) long creature with red legs and a wasp waist, lays its eggs in the body of that notorious pest of vegetable gardens, the caterpillar of the cabbage white butterfly. Within a few days tiny maggots hatch out, and proceed to eat their way through the meal of fresh meat provided by the flesh of the caterpillar, which is helpless to defend itself and is condemned to die a lingering death as it is eaten away bit by bit, till nothing is left of it but the skin. After they have gorged themselves on their dying 'host' (as naturalists call the unwilling victim), the ichneumon grubs pupate in small golden-yellow cases, which can often be seen on fences or walls, sometimes with the remains of the caterpillar skin among them.

There are several other useful parasites, particularly the small wasp-like creatures known as chalcids. One species, *Pteromalus puparum*, also preys upon the young of the cabbage white butterfly, but waits till the caterpillar has turned into a chrysalis. While the newly formed chrysalis is still soft-skinned the female chalcid carefully places an egg at a vulnerable spot. She only has to lay one egg per chrysalis, because each of her eggs divides many times, to produce a mass of tiny wriggling grubs, each with a passion for caterpillar meat.

BIOLOGICAL CONTROL

So far, we have dealt with those useful pest-destroying creatures that appear among our plants by lucky chance. Nowadays, however, a thriving business is being built up by research stations and private firms using mass-production methods to produce and market specially reared parasites to control pests. Progressive commercial growers have been buying and using these mass-produced parasites for years, especially to protect glasshouse crops, and getting excellent results. Now production is being stepped up, and increasing quantities of parasites are being bought by the public. More and more gardeners prefer them to the poisonous chemicals which are becoming an increasing source of worry to thoughtful people concerned about the effects of such poisons both on the environment and on their own health. So far only a few pests have been controlled by purpose-bred parasites in this way, but research is going on all the time, and within a few years we may expect to see a whole new range of parasitical pest-destroyers.

Since there is no living thing, animal or vegetable, that is not preyed on by parasites of one sort or another, it is possible that for every bad bug we shall one day be able to buy a good bug specially produced to control it. Then perhaps the manufacturers of chemical poisons will start to see their business and their profits take a dive – unless, that is, they have the commercial sense to start switching to the production of parasites and predators.

The distinction between the two is a simple one. A predator may seem to the squeamish rather less disgusting, because it kills its victim and then eats it. A parasite, on the other hand, eats its victim alive, and may go to some lengths to keep it alive to the last possible moment. Females of many species inject the victim with a paralysing fluid before laying their eggs, not only to render it helpless but to preserve its flesh alive till the last grub has eaten its fill; the young parasites instinctively avoid the vital organs, so as not to kill the host before they have finished with it.

Whitefly parasites

Among the pest-killers commercially introduced during the past few years, one of the most successful is the whitefly parasite,

Encarsia formosa, a tiny wasp, about a sixteenth of an inch (1.5 mm) long, with a yellow and black body. Each adult female lives for about three weeks, during which she lays fifty or sixty eggs; she inserts each of them singly into a whitefly scale. Several days later the egg hatches out into a minute grub, which feeds on the flesh of the young whitefly inside the scale. After the parasite grub has eaten enough whitefly meat to become fully grown, it pupates inside the scale, which turns black. In two or three weeks it develops into an adult, which cuts a neat hole in the scale, struggles out, dries its wings, and flies off. The parasites are sold in the form of black scales on pieces of leaf. Hang up the pieces of leaf among your plants, and in a few days holes will appear in the black scales, showing that the adult wasps have emerged.

Some people worry about what will happen to the parasites after they have eaten all the whitefly scales. Will they, if there is none of their usual food left, turn into pests themselves and start attacking plants – or even people? The answer is no. The digestive system of the parasite is not able to cope with anything but the flesh of young whitefly; without that the parasite will starve to death.

That is, indeed, one of the problems of biological control: the more efficient a parasite or predator is at destroying a pest, the sooner it will itself die out for want of food. One hundred per cent efficiency in eradicating the pest will very soon be followed by 100 per cent death of the parasites; so that if another attack by the same pest should occur later, a fresh lot of parasites will have to be bought. The best natural balance is obtained when enough of the pests survive to provide food to keep a few parasites alive.

You should start using the parasites early in the season, while the whitefly are few in number. If too many whitefly build up before the encarsia can get to work on them, you may have to spray with an insecticide to keep them down to manageable numbers. In any case some other pest such as greenfly may appear which the parasite cannot tackle, and which must therefore be dealt with by an insecticide. Unfortunately many of the powerful modern chemicals are even more lethal to parasites and predators than they are to pests, so you should use one that does the least harm to them, such as pirimicarb, derris or pyrethrum.

Red spider predators

The most effective killer of that serious greenhouse pest the red spider mite is another mite, remarkably like it in appearance, called *Phytoseiulus persimilis*. Like the whitefly parasite, the red spider predator is supplied on pieces of leaf, accompanied by enough red spider mites to keep it fed during its journey to you, because unlike the whitefly parasite it comes to you as a fully active creature with a ravenous appetite. It is shiny in appearance and red in colour – redder indeed than most of the so-called red spiders, which are often straw-coloured. It can eat eight or nine red spiders, or up to twenty of their eggs, a day; and over a period of about three weeks it lays some fifty eggs, which hatch out very quickly into hungry youngsters, scurrying about in search of their prey.

The pieces of leaf carrying the predators are placed on infested plants, and within a few minutes the predator will have run on to the plant and started tucking into the feast of red spiders ready prepared for it. The only snag is that the predator is almost too efficient a pest-eater for its own good. The usual package, when opened, is found to contain four or five pieces of leaf, carrying enough predators – together with eggs laid in transit, which will hatch out in a day or two – to search out and eat every red spider and red spider's egg in an average greenhouse within three or four weeks. After this, the predator faces starvation.

Germ warfare

As a further development of biological control, a great deal of study is being devoted to diseases that attack insect pests, so that by infecting a pest with its own special disease it may be killed – or so severely damaged that it cannot eat or breed – with no risk whatever to people, other animals, or even other insects. It is now possible to culture, by laboratory methods, germs that cause disease among greenfly and other aphids, so as to produce an extremely virulent strain; the resulting spray is highly infectious to aphids but completely harmless to other creatures. The beauty of this method is that it does not stop with the death of the aphids on which the spray has been used: each corpse will release more germs to infect further aphids, and each of these will in turn infect still more, until an epidemic of plague proportions has broken loose throughout the aphid population.

A thoroughly tested and proved strain that brings disease and death to caterpillars is already in widespread use among commercial growers, and supplies are beginning to be obtainable from some garden centres and stores. The product is sold as a wettable powder; mixed with water and sprayed so as to cover the leaves completely every ten days or so, it gives highly effective protection throughout the season. Since the germ does not attack human beings, the manufacturers of the product quite correctly claim that it does not taint edible crops, which can be harvested and used straight away. Though this is true, it is still a good idea to wait for a few days after spraying before gathering the crop. The reason is that large caterpillars may take four or five days to die and fall off the plant; until they do, you are liable to gather dying caterpillars among the crop.

Is there any danger, you may ask, that deliberately introduced germs may start spreading disease to other creatures besides caterpillars? The answer is no. Disease germs are incapable of infecting dissimilar types of organism. There is, however, one unfortunate and unpleasant feature of the product just described. Wonderful though it may be at destroying caterpillars, it has a quite outstandingly disgusting smell: not just the nasty chemical smell associated with ordinary insecticides, but an overpowering stench, hard to describe but foul beyond words. Fortunately it soon fades, but it is nauseating while it lasts.

Experiments with other diseases that attack plant pests are going on in laboratories all the time. Germ warfare of this kind, directed only at foes and leaving friends unscathed, should provide a much better answer to the problems of pest control than the present methods of chemical warfare.

Birth control

All attempts to control pests, whether by chemicals or by germs, are bound to have limited success, since by the normal process of natural selection new strains of the pest are sure to appear which are resistant to existing pesticides and diseases. More lethal chemicals and germs must then be found, which will result in even more resistant pests, and so the process will go on. If, however, an effective system of birth control for pests could be devised, the problem would be solved.

A considerable amount of research has been done on ways of stopping pests producing families, or at the least severely restricting family size. Experiments have been made with chemicals designed to interfere with the normal reproductive cycle of female insects, similar in action to The Pill on human females. The results have been patchy, ranging from failure to produce eggs at all to the laying of eggs that were either infertile or hatched out into defective offspring, unable to survive, or if they did survive unable to reproduce.

Some experiments have been made by sterilizing females in the laboratory and then letting them loose, to draw the attention of amorous males and make sure that no little pests result from the mating. On the whole, though, sterilizing females does not seem to be a very practical method of contraception, since there will always be large numbers of unsterilized females about in the wild.

A more promising contraceptive technique being developed at present is to sterilize large quantities of males and then release them among the wild female population, to mate with them without fertilizing them. The timing has to be exactly right, or the available females will already have been seduced by wild males with their reproductive faculties intact. What experimental laboratories are working on at the moment is the breeding of superstud male pests, stronger, faster and more virile than their wild rivals, which will not stand a chance against them in competing for females. These superstuds will then be sterilized and let loose, to indulge their sexual appetites without begetting offspring.

PEST-EATING PLANTS

One method of pest control is to use carnivorous plants for the purpose. There are over 450 species at present known which feed on insects.

Venus's fly-trap

The most spectacular are those with 'jaws' which snap shut on their prey, such as the Venus's fly-trap, *Dionaea muscipula*, a native of Carolina, which is sold by some garden suppliers as a kind of plant pet, always ready to perform its trick for the pleasure of its owner or visitors. The triangular leaves end in traps, hinged together along the middle and fringed with a row of formidable-looking teeth. Each half of the trap carries three bristle-like trigger hairs, and when an unwary fly, attracted by the nectar secreted inside the edges, touches these hairs, the two jaws snap together in a split second, the teeth meshing with each other so as to stop the victim escaping. Within a day or two, the soft parts of the fly are digested by means of a fluid secreted from special glands, and the trap opens again, to eject the insect's skeleton and to lie in wait for the next victim.

Pitfalls for pests

Another type of trap is used by various species of pitcher-plant to catch their prey. It has no moving parts and does not snap shut, but consists of a funnel-like vessel with nectar-secreting glands around the rim. Attracted by the nectar, insects venture inside, lose their foothold, and tumble into the liquid at the bottom of the pitcher, where they are soon digested. Several species of pitcher-plant are quite hardy and will grow outside in a bog garden, but neither they nor the species from warmer climates which are sometimes grown in greenhouses are easy to manage in mixed collections of plants, and they are unlikely to get rid of more than a very few of the insect pests that plague gardeners.

Living fly-papers

Less dramatic in their methods, but very effective at catching, killing and eating insects, are those carnivorous plants that rely on sticky surfaces which grab and hold on to small struggling creatures till they can struggle no more. Typical of these living fly-papers are the sundews, of which over ninety species are known throughout the world, ranging in size from the miniature *Drosera pygmaea*, less than ½ inch (12.5 mm) high, to *Drosera gigantea*, which can reach as much as 3 feet (90 cm), and is able to ensnare quite large insects. The leaves are covered with reddish hairs tipped with glands which exude a sticky, sugary fluid, very attractive to flies and other small creatures. When the visitor, having imbibed enough, decides the time has come to move on, it finds it cannot, and its desperate attempts to break away only bring it into contact with yet more sticky hairs, which hold it more tightly than ever. Other sensitive hairs, able to detect the food substances in the insect, curl over the victim and wrap themselves around it. The last dying movements of the prey stimulate the glands to produce digestive juices, which break down the softer parts of the insect, leaving only the dry husk of the victim to be blown away by the wind when the leaf opens out again to catch the next meal.

Many species of sundew are completely hardy through the bitterest winter. Some are native to wet places throughout the British Isles, and may be grown successfully out of doors in the bog garden. Sundews in cultivation, however, are best grown in greenhouses, where they will help to catch and dispose of any pests that might find their way in. Most species carry purple, violet or scarlet flowers, but those of the commonest British species, *Drosera rotundifolia*, are a somewhat dirty white. The most popular greenhouse species from abroad, *Drosera binata*, has larger, whiter and altogether more attractive flowers, and although it comes from Australia it seems to have no objection to a diet of British insects.

Grease-traps

Perhaps the most effective 'fly-paper plant' in cultivation is the butterwort, *Pinguicula*, so called because of the greasy appearance of its leaves, which look as if they have been smeared with butter (the botanical name comes from the Latin *pinguis*, meaning fat). Several hardy species can be grown in boggy soil in the garden, not merely for the interest of their insect-eating habits but also for their attractive, long-spurred flowers in shades of violet, lilac, pale blue and sometimes white, with markings on the lips and in the throat. Two very beautiful species come from America: *Pinguicula lutea*, native to the south-eastern United States from North Carolina to Florida, with bright orange-yellow flowers, and *Pinguicula bakerana*, from Mexico, with flowers of a most intense carmine. Both these species need the protection of a greenhouse, where they are remarkably efficient in dealing with any insects rash or unlucky enough to come in contact with the greasy-looking leaves. So powerful is the action of their digestive juices that in some places the leaves are gathered by country people and used to curdle milk.

GOOD COMPANIONS

Many plants are believed to go particularly well together, so that when they grow side by side each benefits from the other. Sweeping claims have been made about these 'companion plants', and some seedsmen are developing a profitable sideline by offering in their catalogues, alongside some of their best sellers, small packets of seed of companion plants which, the blurb alleges, will protect the crop from pests and/or disease.

Unfortunately there is so far very little real evidence of the effectiveness or otherwise of these chosen companions (though there is considerable evidence of the sales-effectiveness of the carefully chosen words of the blurb). At present about the only thing that can be said with certainty is that rarely if ever in a natural environment is one species of plant found growing on its own; there is always a mixed community of different kinds, growing in close proximity and interacting with each other. Only under human cultivation can be found large areas of ground given over to only one kind of plant, such as wheat, sugar beet, or potatoes. This single-crop production – monoculture, as it is called – can lead to total disaster if a pest or disease specific to that crop should attack in force. It then becomes essential for the grower to spray or dust ever more frequently and with ever more powerful chemicals as resistant strains of the pest or disease develop.

If the growing of other plants among the main crop could ward off the attack, that would obviously be a great advantage to everyone (except the chemical manufacturers). No commercial grower can afford to experiment with unproved methods, however; nor can the large research stations, most of which are financed at the taxpayer's expense or by the chemical manufacturers themselves. This is where the amateur gardener, whose livelihood is not at stake, can take a chance and do a little experimenting to see whether any of these plant associations really do work.

If you should decide to try the effect of companion plants, the vegetable garden is probably the best place to make a start, because (a) vegetables are particularly prone to attack by pests and diseases, (b) not being permanent crops, vegetables can be rearranged with different companion plants from season to season, and (c) there seems to be more folklore about vegetables and herbs than about other plants. If your experiments are to be of any value, you must leave some of your vegetables without the companion plant, just as a doctor testing the effects of a drug will leave a control group of patients without the drug, so as to be able to compare results between the treated and untreated groups.

How one plant might benefit another

There would seem to be three ways in which one kind of plant might benefit another kind growing near it. First, it could send out substances – from its roots, its leaves or its flowers – that kill or repel organisms harmful to the other plant. It is often asserted, for instance, that French marigolds, *Tagetes patula*, give out secretions from their roots that can destroy, at a distance of as much as 3 feet (90 cm), the eelworms which do so much damage to many species of plant, particularly potatoes and tomatoes. It is also asserted that their leaves and flowers give off vapours which keep whitefly away. The same claim is made for the closely related but taller and larger-flowered African marigold, *Tagetes erecta* (which, by the way, no more comes from Africa than French marigolds come from France: they are both natives of Mexico). Both these species are half-hardy annuals, with attractive flowers in shades of yellow, gold and orange, and both have long been grown in our gardens for their ornamental value; it is only recently that their supposed virtues as pest-repellents have been publicized.

Many gardeners nowadays are growing these French and African marigolds as companion plants among their tomatoes; some people swear by them and claim to have conquered the pest problem with their help, while others say they make no difference – or even, after finding swarms of whitefly on the marigolds themselves, that they make matters worse. The latest claims are being made for a different species, *Tagetes minuta*, which comes from South America (where the tomato also originated, possibly – who knows? – in association with it). This is said to be much more effective in controlling whitefly than either French or African marigolds. It might be worth trying, but unfortunately ordinary seedsmen do not stock it, because the small, pallid, insignificant flowers are of no decorative value at all. Its other disadvantage is that it grows tall and untidy (in spite of the word *minuta*, meaning tiny, which refers to the size of the flowers, not the plant).

Many other plants are said to send out vapours that repel insect pests. Basil, for instance, with its warm, pungent scent, is claimed to be the perfect companion for tomato plants, warding off attacks by whitefly and preventing moths from laying the eggs which hatch into destructive caterpillars. Other people assert that the ideal companion for tomatoes is the nasturtium (called *Tropaeolum* by botanists), which is alleged to produce strong aromatic substances that pass not only into the air but into the soil too, where they are taken up by the roots of the tomato plants into the fruit, which they make unpalatable to insects. The smell of onions growing next to carrots is said by many to deter the carrot fly, whose grubs can completely ruin the crop by tunnelling into the roots; at the same time the onion fly, it is claimed, cannot stand the smell of carrots, and goes off to lay its eggs on somebody else's onions instead. For this reason, some people have taken to growing alternate rows of carrots and onions in their vegetable gardens.

There is no doubt that many pests have their strong likes and dislikes in the way of scents; indeed, it is their sense of smell that guides them to their particular food-plant, which is usually the only thing they can digest. It is argued, therefore, that if instead of growing many rows of the same crop together several different kinds are interspersed with each other, insects will become thoroughly confused. One smell will beckon invitingly, but at the same time another will repel, and so the pest, torn between attraction and repulsion, will fly off to find another garden where things are not so confusing.

The second way in which one plant might benefit another growing near it is by actually giving up some of its own food for its companion's use. Sometimes the donor gets something back in return, as in the case of the lichens, those growths that form coloured crusts on rocks, walls, roofs and trunks of trees. They are not one plant but two, a fungus and an alga living together in a prolonged intimate embrace, one taking material from the surface where they are growing and the other from the air, and building those materials into food for them both. This sort of interdependence, known as *symbiosis* (from the Greek 'living together'), takes many forms. The tiny seeds of orchids, for instance, as fine as face-powder, do not contain the food reserves of ordinary seeds, and so can only grow if they are given sugar, and this is provided in nature by a special companion fungus.

A well-known example of symbiosis, of considerable importance to vegetable-growers, is the way in which certain bacteria invade the roots of leguminous plants (peas, beans and the like) and cause warty swellings, called nodules, which might be mistaken for the symptoms of some disease. Far from causing disease, however, the microbes inhabiting the nodules are busy extracting nitrogen from the air and turning it into nitrogenous fertilizer, which in return for their board and lodging they feed to the plant. In turn the leguminous crops enrich the soil with the nitrogenous compounds thus provided by the bacteria and so pass on food for other plants. That is why peas and beans are able not only to thrive on nitrogen-starved soil but to improve its fertility.

The third way in which companion plants may get along well with each other is by having different food requirements, so that the first can feed heavily on one food element without depriving the second, whose appetite for that element is slight – though it may need a substantial amount of another element that the first hardly wants at all. It is this different appetite of different plants for different foods that is one of the chief reasons why it is best to change the position of the main crops in the vegetable garden each season. Another reason is that switching around helps to prevent what can become a catastrophic build-up of pests and diseases in the soil.

Unlike chemical fertilizers and pesticides, companion plants can hardly do much harm even if they do little good (though some plants are said to be antagonistic towards each other). If the subject interests you further, you can buy books devoted solely to companion plants, dealing in detail with their supposed likes and dislikes. Some of the recommended interplantings – for instance, potatoes sharing their bed with cabbages, beans, marigolds, sweet corn and horse-radish – may not seem very practical, but some of the easier ones – such as lettuce with radish, or carrots with onions – may be worth trying. Above all, take the assertions made in such books with a large pinch of salt. If you find a crop attacked by the very pest that the companion plant was supposed to ward off, believe your eyes, not the books, and use an appropriate insecticide quickly, before the situation gets out of hand.

COMMON PESTS

Having dealt with some of the gardener's many animal and vegetable friends, we must now turn our attention to the less pleasant subject of the enemies, usually divided into pests on the one hand and diseases on the other. The distinction, though, is not very clear or precise, since all the things that attack plants are alike in their capacity to spread and reproduce themselves, even those ultra-microscopic agents of disease, the viruses, or 'living chemicals'.

One distinction commonly assumed is that pests can be seen with the naked eye whereas disease organisms need a microscope. Probably a truer distinction is that the pests that attack plants are animals, whereas the vast majority of plant diseases are caused by other plants, usually of the lowly kind known as fungi, which, having no chlorophyll with which to build themselves, have turned parasite and steal their nourishment by sucking it from other living things. Diseases, mainly fungoid in origin, are dealt with under 'Ailments' (pages 207–10), and pests, all animal, are dealt with here. We will start with pests that attack a wide range of different plants, and then go on to specialist pests that confine their unwelcome attentions to one kind of plant – sometimes a few species, and sometimes one species only.

Feathered foes

We started our list of the gardener's best friends with birds (see page 170). But some birds, sometimes, do a good deal of damage. Many of them include seeds as a favourite item in their diet, and can cause havoc in a seed-bed by scratching up the ground and eating the seeds you have just sown. Even birds that have no particular taste for seeds can be almost as much of a nuisance by taking a dust-bath in your carefully raked soil, which is just what they like, especially on a hot day. Some spring flowers such as crocus and polyanthus can be torn to shreds by birds. Black threads stretched above the plants and supported on short sticks stuck into the ground will scare the birds off by snatching at them without doing them any harm. In the vegetable garden rows of tiny seedlings can be protected by covering them with lengths of small-mesh wire netting bent up along the middle.

Much more severe damage is done to soft fruit – especially strawberries, raspberries and red currants – which may be stripped, particularly in the early morning before anyone is up and about to frighten the birds away. The only satisfactory answer is to enclose the soft fruit in a cage, covered with ¾-inch (20 mm) netting. Any wider mesh will let the birds in, or worse still half in, so that they get stuck by the neck, leaving you to try to disentangle the flapping, terrified creatures; sometimes one may even strangle itself before you find it. Excellent portable cages are obtainable, with a framework of uprights and cross-pieces of tubular galvanized steel, which are easily slotted into each other, and can be quickly dismantled and stored away after the fruit has been picked, allowing the birds to get at the ground and do a useful job of eating pests instead of fruit.

The same cage can be put over vegetables of the cabbage family – Brussels sprouts, cauliflower, broccoli and kale – during the winter to keep off hungry pigeons, which can quickly reduce leaves to skeletons. A warning is needed, however. If it snows, the ¾-inch (20 mm) roof net that was needed in the summer will unfortunately be fine enough to trap the snow, which will soon become so heavy that it breaks the net. A special anti-pigeon net must therefore be used for the roof, of much wider mesh (4 inches (10 cm) is best), which will let the snow through – and for that matter the small birds – but keep the pigeons out.

If you can afford it, buy a cage tall enough for you to stand up in, preferably with a door, which does not cost much extra. Then you will not have to grovel about on your hands and knees, and fruit-picking will become a pleasant occupation instead of a back-breaking chore.

Where tree fruits are concerned, cages are not a practical proposition. Individual fruits, or bunches of fruit, may be given some protection by enclosing them in polythene bags, but that is a tedious job, and in any case the birds will soon discover that they can peck through the polythene to get at the fruit. Various scaring devices have been tried to keep the birds away: the old-fashioned scarecrow (which soon becomes a figure of contempt, and is used as a perching place by the more venturesome birds); strips of metal foil, hung from branches or posts to dance and glitter in the sun; slivers of glass, arranged to tinkle as well as glisten; and lengths of hosepipe arranged to look like snakes. Some people place bits of mirror in trees, the idea being that the bird will attack its reflection rather than the fruit. Unfortunately it is impossible to explain the idea to the birds, which tend to ignore the mirror and go for the fruit.

The most severe and widespread damage is that inflicted early in the season by bud-eating birds, especially the bullfinch, which looks so pretty and innocent but is actually a dedicated and enthusiastic vandal, capable of pecking out every single bud from a fruit tree with ruthless efficiency. Ornamental trees and bushes such as prunus and forsythia are also stripped of buds. It is extremely difficult to prevent such attacks, since a full-sized tree is impossible to net efficiently. Commercial fruit-growers sometimes, in desperation, use traps to catch the birds, but the success rate is usually not very high. Other devices which have been tried include recorded alarm calls of bullfinches played over loudspeakers, life-size models of hawks and owls kept hovering in the air on the end of long poles or suspended from balloons, and even fur hats placed on branches in the hope that the birds will mistake them for cats. None of these devices seems to work for long. Birds soon get used to them and refuse to be made fools of. To be bird-brained is not necessarily to be stupid.

A few years ago it looked as if the problem had been overcome by the development of a fine rayon web, which when festooned over the trees in early spring when the buds begin to swell would cause birds to keep away for fear of getting entangled. After the danger period was over, it was claimed that the rayon web would soon rot away and disappear through the action of weather. The snag was that the weather could not be relied upon to be bad enough, so during a long fine spell the rayon strands would remain intact, and by cutting into the new growth as the buds expanded could cause almost as much damage as the birds themselves.

Some success is claimed for the use of bird-repellent sprays based on chemicals such as anthraquinone, which make the buds unpalatable. The spray must be applied early in the year, just when the buds are beginning to swell, and it is important that the process should be repeated several times, both when heavy rain washes the spray off and when the buds expand, shedding their scales and the protective chemical covering with them.

Finally, try keeping a cat. There is nothing more effective for scaring off birds; even the sight of it lying curled up fast asleep may be enough to keep marauders at bay. The only problem is that if the cat has a nice warm home it may be reluctant to spend much time outside in the garden during the cold days at the critical period when the buds are starting to swell.

Rabbits

Rabbits can do a tremendous amount of damage to young growth. The vegetable garden provides them with just the tender, juicy young produce they like most, but they can also do a lot of damage in the flower-beds and borders, particularly early in the season, by nibbling off the new growth as it starts to appear. If rabbits get at young trees they may gnaw the bark, which they greatly enjoy. Sometimes they strip it off, and so kill the tree. If there is a bad infestation of rabbits in your neighbourhood, get on to your local council; they have – or should have – a department equipped to deal with such things.

For young trees, it is possible to buy rabbit guards, or you can make quite effective protectors by circling the trunk with wire netting. Various repellents are on sale, intended to discourage rabbits by their nasty smell, including pepper dust, which is also claimed to keep off cats and dogs. The only really effective way to protect the vegetable garden is to surround it with a fence of wire netting, sunk deep enough into the ground to prevent the rabbits from burrowing under it, and high enough to stop them from jumping over it.

Slugs and snails

These do widespread and serious damage to young growth. Unfortunately the problem is often made a great deal worse by a tidy, well-kept garden. In natural conditions these pests are largely scavengers, preferring to browse on old, decaying leaves, which they find soft and easy to chew. In well-kept gardens, from which old decaying leaves are scrupulously removed, the slugs and snails cannot find the food they enjoy most, so they settle for what to them is the next best thing – that is to say tender young growth. On a full-grown plant they are quite capable, slow-moving though they are, of climbing to the top to devour the soft growing tips. With young seedlings, particularly of tender-leaved vegetables such as lettuce, where there is no climbing to do, a single fair-sized slug or snail can polish off a whole row in a night. These pests are often at their worst during damp weather, when the moist soil is more comfortable for them to crawl about on than a dry, gritty surface. They usually show where they have been by leaving a slimy trail behind them, which may give you the satisfaction of tracking them down to their daytime hiding places – under stones or rubbish, or in shady crevices – and destroying them, even though by then the damage may have been done.

Some people try to keep slugs and snails from attacking precious seedlings by sprinkling sharp grit around the stems or along the rows. There are many brands of slug pellets on the market based on metaldehyde, which the pests find tasty and which poisons them after a bite or two. The best of these pellets are treated to make them showerproof and mould-resistant. Though this treatment may make them a little dearer to buy, it really makes them more economical, since their effectiveness lasts much longer.

As with nearly all modern chemical pesticides, resistant strains of the pests occur, and already there are super-slugs that seem to enjoy their meal of metaldehyde slug pellets without suffering any ill effects. To cope with these, a pellet based on the chemical methiocarb has been developed, which is at present highly effective. Some people, anticipating the emergence of strains of slugs and snails that are resistant to the effects of methiocarb, use both sorts of pellet, in the hope that those pests that are not killed by one may be killed by the other.

It is important to go round in the morning to collect up the poisoned slugs and snails, for two reasons: first, they may not be completely dead, and may revive; second, if left about they may poison birds or other friendly creatures that might eat them.

Some people, bothered by the use (and indeed the expense) of chemical baits, dispose of the pests by drowning them in beer. All that is needed is some sort of small container – a cream or yoghurt carton will do – sunk into the ground and filled with beer up to about an inch (2.5 cm) below the rim. The beer acts as a powerful magnet to slugs, which sample it, fall in, and finish up, in a thoroughly literal sense, dead drunk. It is a good idea to cover the container with a stone or something similar, leaving only enough room for slugs to get in, so as to protect the beer from larger creatures such as birds, though neither the drowned slugs nor the beer itself seem to do birds any harm.

Another old-fashioned and non-poisonous device to catch slugs is a trap made of a hollowed-out piece of potato or carrot, placed on, or just below, the surface of the ground. The pests, attracted by the cut surface, will have a good feed and then sleep it off in the hollowed out part. Lift the trap in the morning and dispose of the contents, which may include, besides slugs, a woodlouse or two.

Remember to spare any testacella slugs you may find. As we have seen, they are wholly carnivorous and spend their time eating pests. You can easily recognize them by the small, ear-like shell at their rear end (see page 172).

Mice

These can be very destructive, gnawing almost every part of many different kinds of plant: roots, bulbs and corms, shoots, bark, fruits and seeds. They are particularly fond of newly sown pea and bean seeds, which give them just the high-protein diet they need when they become active in the spring. If one gets in a greenhouse it can be very troublesome indeed, leaving almost nothing in the plant line undamaged.

Peas and beans may be protected from attack to some extent by soaking the seeds in paraffin before sowing, to make them unpalatable, and/or by sprinkling paraffin-soaked sawdust along the rows. Traps can be a help, but put them in a place where pets cannot get caught by them. Placing the trap inside a length of narrow drainpipe is a good method, but watch when you are pushing the set trap along the drainpipe that you do not spring it and get your own fingers caught.

Poison baits based on the chemical coumatetralyl, mixed with bran, grain or some similar feeding stuff, are popular and effective. The bait is made into small heaps, and has to be renewed, or at least topped up, every day, till the mice stop eating it, which means they have crawled away to die somewhere. The process may take several days, the poison being cumulative in its effects. A basin of water placed beside the bait is a good idea, since one of the early effects of the poison is to make the mice intensely thirsty, and unable to take the bait before their thirst is quenched.

Although this poison is supposed to be specific in its action to rats and mice, put it where pets cannot get at it. The simplest way is to place it, like traps, in a piece of drainpipe. If the mice do not seem to be taking the bait enthusiastically enough, try mixing a little sugar with it to make it more attractive.

One way of keeping down mice is to keep a cat. Do not make the mistake of underfeeding the cat in the belief that that will make it catch more mice. A well-fed cat is a much better mouser than a half-starved one.

Cats

In spite of their usefulness in keeping down mice, and bird nuisances too, cats can themselves be a nuisance when they roll about on seed-beds or scratch them up. You can buy canisters of pepper-dust to sprinkle on the ground, which is alleged to keep cats (and for that matter dogs) away because of its smell, but probably the best way of preventing cats making a nuisance of themselves is to put wire-netting over the seed-bed till the seed-lings are well established. This will foil mice and birds as well.

Wireworms

These creatures, the young of click beetles, are thin and wiry, with six legs at the front; they are a dirty cream colour at first but turn brown as they grow. They are normally found in grassland, where they live in the soil and feed on the grass roots and any bits and pieces of organic matter they can find; they continue like this for several years and then turn into adult beetles. In their grassland haunts they are not usually much of a nuisance; indeed, unless they reach plague proportions, they might be said to be beneficial, because by trimming the roots they control the growth and give some check to the coarser-growing grasses, which might take over if not root-pruned in this way.

When old grassland is dug up to make beds and borders, however, which is very often the case with new gardens, or where a lawn has been converted into a vegetable patch, wireworms can be a serious problem. Denied their normal diet of grass roots, they turn their attention to anything else they can find, feeding avidly on roots, bulbs, tubers, corms, and even stems at ground level.

Control of wireworms is not easy. Many people find it best to grow potatoes as a 'cleaning crop' in newly dug grassland for the first year; lift the tubers early in the season and destroy the ones riddled with wireworms. You may even find a few undamaged ones for use in the kitchen, especially if you plant an early variety.

Getting rid of wireworms and other soil pests

Some chemical products, sold under various brand names, help to keep down infestations of wireworms and many other soil pests. Probably the most economically effective is gamma-HCH dust, still often called by the old name BHC, but this must not be used where potatoes or carrots or other root crops are grown, or it will taint them and make them taste foul. Other chemical controls include products containing bromophos, diazinon or chlorpyrifos. However, it appears that some strains of wireworms and other soil pests are now showing marked resistance to these modern insecticides, and many people are going back to older remedies such as naphthalene, which is supposed to put off soil pests by its smell.

Greenhouse border soil is occasionally invaded by wireworms and other soil pests. The best way to avoid this nuisance is to use sterilized soil. The usual method commercial growers use to sterilize their border soil is to steam it; some, though, are going over to methyl bromide, a very dangerous gas which can only be applied by qualified contractors with special equipment and protective clothing. Such treatments are not suitable for amateurs, but there are some effective chemical soil sterilants obtainable in small packs from garden suppliers. Basamid is one of the easiest to use, but since it releases toxic fumes into the soil it must be treated with respect and caution; follow the instructions on the pack to the letter, and take particular care to allow the stated time to elapse before planting is done, to make sure the fumes have completely dispersed.

Leatherjackets

These plump, grey, wrinkled and legless larvae of the crane-fly, or daddy-long-legs, do a great deal of damage in the soil, specializing in nipping off stems just below the surface. Often the first sign of attack is the sudden wilting of a plant; on examination it is found to have been severed from all or most of its roots. Leatherjackets enjoy rather damp earth, so good drainage may discourage them. Many birds find them delicious, so where ground is infested with them – especially newly turned grassland, where they often congregate, rather like wireworms – dig it over before the end of September, so as to leave the grubs exposed to hungry beaks. For chemical methods of control see the previous paragraph.

Cutworms

This name is given to the caterpillars of several different kinds of moth, varying in colour from dirty white to greenish grey. They live near the surface of the soil and come out at night to feed, which they do by the simple process of cutting off young plants at ground level. A hungry cutworm or two can destroy a whole row of promising seedlings in a night. Perhaps the most effective, and personally satisfying, way of dealing with them is to go out with a torch at night and catch them in the act. If you prefer to look for them by day, you may find them under a nearby stone or lump of earth sleeping off the effects of their meal. Since cutworms feed on many different kinds of weeds as well as cultivated plants, it is important to keep weeds down in order to deny the pests food and

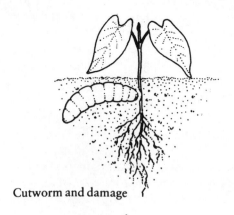

Cutworm and damage

refuge. Experiments are at present being carried out in the use of disease as a weapon against cutworms, as has already been done successfully with other types of caterpillar (see page 180). Results are promising, but the method has not yet been sufficiently developed to be generally available. For chemical methods of control see p. 195.

Chafer grubs

These revolting-looking creatures are large, fat, soft and curved, with brown heads. Their bodies are unhealthy and pallid in appearance; they look as if they have crawled out from under a stone, which they probably have. They gorge themselves on the roots of growing plants 2 inches (5 cm) or more below the surface of the soil, and can cause very severe damage. Eventually they turn into adult beetles, of which the three commonest species are the cockchafer, the garden chafer and the rose chafer. These adult beetles, brown or green in colour and up to an inch (2.5 cm) long, chew holes in leaves, shoots, flowers and fruits, though usually the damage they cause is not so bad as that caused by their young.

As with other soil pests, try to keep the ground free from weeds to deny both the grubs and the adults food and shelter. The grubs are not always easy to find, since they can go down to quite a depth. If, however, you suspect their presence because of the wilting of a plant, dig around and you may be rewarded by finding and destroying one or two. For chemical methods of control see p. 195. Adult beetles may be picked off plants by hand and disposed of; or you can spray with an anti-beetle insecticide, such as one containing carbaryl.

Millipedes

Sometimes called black wireworms, these dark-coloured creatures have rounded bodies with usually two pairs of legs to a segment. They curl up into coils when resting or when disturbed, and hatch out from eggs laid in the soil. They live largely on decaying vegetable matter, but also attack the underground parts of living plants – roots, bulbs and tubers – which they riddle with holes during their somewhat messy eating, opening the way to disease. If the soil near damaged plants is examined, the culprits may be found curled up in the earth, or sometimes in the attacked parts of the plants; tubers of underground crops such as potatoes are specially vulnerable. For chemical means of control see p. 195.

Do not confuse millipedes with the wholly excellent and helpful centipedes, which are splendid pest-destroyers and should never be killed. It is perfectly easy to tell the two different kinds of creatures apart (see page 174).

Whiteflies

These extremely troublesome pests have been increasing in number during the past few years, largely because many modern insecticides kill the creatures that used to prey on them. Though whiteflies look rather like tiny moths, they are actually related to the aphids, or plant lice, and to the scale insects, and they have the nastier habits of both. They weaken all kinds of plants, particularly soft-leaved vegetables such as tomatoes and cucumbers, by sucking the sap. In doing so they exude a sticky substance known as honey-dew, which not only clogs up the pores of the leaves but soon gets covered by a fungus called sooty mould, which turns everything black. Though the sooty mould is not particularly harmful it is very unsightly, so that tomatoes covered with it have to be carefully washed before they look fit to eat.

Whiteflies can breed at a fantastic rate, especially in protected situations such as greenhouses. If they are allowed to multiply unchecked, they can soon become almost uncontrollable. They congregate in swarms on the undersides of leaves, particularly at the growing tips of plants, and if disturbed they fly up in a white cloud. They lay masses of tiny eggs, which they attach to the leaves; these hatch out within a few days, and the young go through a period as 'scales', tiny oval affairs fringed with hairs, which attach themselves tightly to the undersides of leaves and suck out the sap till they have had their fill. They then emerge as adult whiteflies to start the whole grisly cycle over again.

Since they have a white, waxy protective covering, they are quite difficult to kill with ordinary chemical sprays. Recently, however, a new range of sprays has been developed based on resmethrin, a chemical closely related to the natural insecticide produced by pyrethrum and similar plants, which has proved effective against whitefly. Unfortunately resistant strains of the pest have already appeared, and slight variations of the chemical formula of these synthetic pyrethroids, as they are called, have been developed, with names like biomethrin, permethrin and decamethrin, to find ever more effective killers and keep one jump ahead of the pests.

The important thing is to spray early in the season, before the whitefly have reached such proportions that it is almost impossible to cope with them. If you prefer to try a biological method of control, you can buy parasitic wasps that live on whitefly, as explained fully on page 177.

Earwigs

Though the old wives' tales that earwigs get into children's ears and send them mad seem to have been discredited, there is no doubt that these creatures can do a considerable amount of damage among plants. This is a great pity, because on the whole

Earwig damage

they are beneficial insects, living mainly on a diet of aphids and other small pests. If only they would stick to being carnivores they could be welcomed as friends of the gardener, but they will insist on being part-time vegetarians as well. They have a particularly annoying habit of climbing into the heads of flowers like dahlias and chrysanthemums and chewing the tips, sometimes completely ruining their looks and robbing them of any decorative value. The well-known common earwig, *Forficula auricularia*, with that formidable-looking pair of pincers at its rear end, also has the maddening habit of cutting neat round holes in apples and other fruit just as they are ripening, not only spoiling their appearance but often causing them to rot.

Since the earwig does not fly, it can be stopped from climbing trees by circling the trunk with a grease band or with a strip of sacking or other material impregnated with smelly insecticide. Where flowers are concerned, the earwigs may be shaken off and disposed of; for really bad infestations, try spraying or dusting with a product containing gamma-HCH (still commonly called BHC), directing the insecticide at the soil and lower parts of the plant. This may need to be done at weekly intervals during the flowering season, starting just before the first flower-buds open, to prevent the earwigs from crawling inside.

Cuckoo-spit bugs

These are the young of a species of froghopper (*Philaenus spumarius*), which as an adult is a dry, hard creature, able to make spectacular, frog-like leaps in the air when disturbed. The young bugs, which are greenish yellow, sometimes with a pinkish tinge, smother themselves with a white froth in which they live, sucking the plant juices. They are very common pests of several garden plants, such as roses, lavender, asters and many others. The frothy masses of 'spit' on young shoots and flower-stalks look somewhat unsightly, and enable visitors and neighbours to do a bit of tut-tutting and express patronizing sympathy. The damage to the plant is usually slight, however, so little or no harm will be done if you ignore the bugs and decide to live and let live. If the infestation is exceptionally bad, or you are exceptionally tidy-minded, you can control the bugs by hosing or spraying with a powerful jet of water to wash off the spit and then either picking off the creatures and squashing them or spraying with a suitable insecticide such as gamma-HCH or malathion.

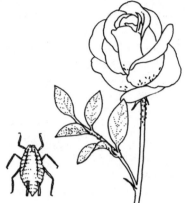

Cuckoo spit: adult and
froth-hidden young

Rose aphid and colony

Aphids

Without doubt, these are the most widespread of all garden pests, and there is almost no plant that escapes their attention. Commonly known as plant lice, or simply by that vague name 'the blight', aphids form a vast family, including greenflies, blackflies, and grey, yellow, brown, red and pink kinds. They not only seriously weaken plants by sucking their sap, but as they puncture the skin to extract the juices they can infect the plants with all kinds of diseases, just as blood-sucking mosquitoes can infect human beings with malaria and other illnesses. Like whiteflies, aphids of many different kinds excrete a sticky, sweet substance called honey-dew which may cover leaves and stems and which in its turn becomes covered with tiny fungi called sooty moulds.

No part of a plant is safe from attack by aphids, which may infest leaves, shoots, flowers and roots, and which may cause all sorts of different symptoms, from leaf-curling to distortion of growing shoots and flowers. Aphids are in every way serious pests, and must be taken seriously if you want to get decent results from your gardening efforts.

The life-style and sexual behaviour of the aphis are somewhat strange and can be very complicated. Eggs are laid on the plant to be attacked, and these eggs hatch out into immature females, known as nymphs. These quickly grow bigger, shedding a few outgrown skins in the process, and soon become wingless adults, which immediately go into labour and start to produce living young. These in turn soon produce living young themselves, by a process of virgin birth, so a heavy infestation can soon build up. Finally winged females are produced, which fly to other plants to start a new colony.

Because aphids are the commonest of pests, there are probably more products sold to fight them than to control any other pest, and since there are so many different species of aphis, each with its own method of attacking its particular host plant, not all of them are equally vulnerable to the same insecticide. Besides, new strains of the pests keep appearing which are resistant to some of the chemicals used against them.

For this reason, it is a good idea to switch from time to time between the various products sold for the control of aphids. No strain has yet appeared that is resistant to all the different anti-aphis products; that remains a nightmare for the future.

Some highly effective chemicals against aphids are only suitable for use by the professional, because they are dangerous unless special equipment is used and stringent precautions taken. There are, however, plenty of perfectly good products available for the amateur, which pose no problems *if they are used strictly in accordance with the makers' instructions*. Among the best are those containing the systemic insecticides dimethoate or for-mothion, which have the advantage that when sprayed on the plant they need not wet the aphids to kill them; the reason they are called systemic is that they are absorbed into the plant's system and pass into the sap-stream, so that when one of the pests punctures the plant's skin and sucks the juice it gives itself a poison drink, which quickly kills it.

For those who are bothered about poisoning the sap-stream with systemic insecticides, especially where edible crops are concerned, there are several effective contact aphicides available, which kill the pests through the skin. Even with these, though, certain plants may be damaged, and an interval of up to two weeks may be needed between spraying and eating fruit and vegetables. Among these contact aphicides, some of the most efficient are those containing malathion, oxydemeton, or pirimi-carb. Safest, even if not quite so efficient, are the 'natural' products produced from plants, derris and pyrethrum. Still at the development stage, and not yet available to amateurs, are concoctions of virulent strains of disease which when sprayed on to aphids can infect and kill them, as explained on page 179.

A remarkable new method of dealing with aphids relies not on poisoning them or infecting them with disease but on getting them confused. During research into the way they fly and what guides them to the plants they attack, strips of aluminium foil were laid, shiny side up, on the ground beside rows of vulnerable crops such as potatoes, which are particularly harmed by aphids because of the virus and other diseases they carry. It was found that the reflected light from the foil caused the aphids to fly upwards into the air instead of downwards on to the plants, apparently mistaking the foil for the sky. Foiled by the foil, they flew off to other places.

Suckers and biters

Having dealt with the commonest of the pests that attack a whole range of young plants, we now come to those which confine their attacks to a single species or to a group of closely related species. The reason for this preference for a monotonous diet is that the pests concerned have an extremely limited digestive system, which can cope with only one kind of vegetable foodstuff. If their particular food plant is not available they will starve to death, even though there is plenty of other vegetation around.

All pests, however specific they are to a particular food plant, belong to one of two kinds: suckers and biters. Suckers, such as aphids, have not been equipped with any means of chewing; like plants themselves, they have to take their nourishment in liquid form, and this they do by penetrating the skin with a device like a hypodermic needle, through which they draw up the plant juices, just like someone sucking a drink through a straw.

Biters, on the other hand, have jaws of one kind or another, which enable them to chew the solid parts of plants, and a digestive system that can cope with solid food. Some biters, such as many types of caterpillar, can chew their way through anything, skin and all, and so leave holes in the plants they attack. Others, like the various leaf miners, cannot manage skin but can only chew the soft inner tissues, so instead of holes they leave

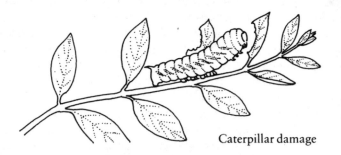

Caterpillar damage

tunnels and blisters. Still others, such as the rose slugworm, can manage skin but not veins, so they eat all the rest of the leaf and leave only a skeleton behind, removing all the green bits and exposing a delicate tracery of veins.

Suckers can be controlled both with contact pesticides and with systemic products. Biters are usually controlled nowadays by contact pesticides, but in some cases may be killed by a poisonous deposit left on the surface of the plant by spraying or dusting.

In using pesticides three things must be remembered. First, pests are amazingly adaptable; as you are reading these words, new strains are no doubt evolving which can survive, and even relish, the chemicals recommended here for their destruction. Second, new products are constantly appearing which are claimed to be – and sometimes are – more effective and/or safer than those previously available. Third, *always read the manufacturer's instructions and follow them to the letter*. Using more than it says on the container in the hope of increasing the effect may – quite apart from the danger to yourself and your family, your pets and your bird and bee visitors – do more harm to the plant than the pest itself would have done.

WEEDS

Many of our most cherished plants, in the garden or the home, are immigrants, brought over by plant-hunters from the ends of the earth; others are highly cultivated varieties of some of our native plants, chosen for some special quality of growth or flower which makes them, in the gardener's eyes, superior to the common run.

Unless something is done to stop it, these strangers would soon be set upon by the rest, who are not only more numerous but usually stronger and coarser.

Left without anything to curb their stronger and coarser nature, weeds would soon give the stranger a very rough time; they were here first, they have over the centuries come to dominate their surroundings, and every natural advantage is on their side. That is why weeds must be controlled. You cannot ignore them; if they were allowed to have their way, your garden would very soon cease to be a garden at all and become instead a wilderness of docks, thistles, nettles, bindweed and coarse grasses. Not only would these crowd out the less aggressive cultivated plants, robbing them of food, light, water and living space, but they act as a breeding ground for pests and diseases, which they are much better able to tolerate than are the cultivated plants. The common weed Shepherd's-purse, for instance, harbours that extremely destructive pest the cabbage root fly. But it does not usually kill the plant, as it often does cabbages and the like, and can be carried over on the weed to attack a new crop next season.

Preventing weeds from winning

Though most weeds can be pretty well controlled nowadays by modern chemical weedkillers, these are quite expensive and may be dangerous to cultivated plants nearby; some have also turned out to be hazardous to human beings and other animals. The very latest weedkillers, such as those containing glyphosate, avoid this danger by being broken down into harmless substances as soon as they come into contact with the soil, so if properly applied they only affect the weeds and nothing else. These, however, are even more expensive, and are only suitable for certain situations, because they can kill every plant they touch; they are therefore useless for lawns.

CHAPTER ELEVEN

Ailments

THE AILMENTS from which young plants suffer are similar to those from which young humans suffer, and can be traced back to the same three basic causes: genetic defects, faulty treatment, and attacks by various pathogens ('germs').

GENETIC DEFECTS

Fortunately, the first of these three factors does not pose the same problems with plants as it does with babies; there are no laws against disposing of handicapped seedlings. So the first step towards having healthy plants is to weed out and destroy the inadequate ones; their remains, while still young and tender, can but put on the compost heap, so their brief lives will not have been entirely wasted. That is the advantage of sowing more seeds than might seem strictly necessary: by leaving only the most robust ones you will be helping the natural process of the survival of the fittest. It must be added that sometimes a particular seedling selected for survival by gardeners may owe its appeal to some genetic defect that might seriously handicap its chances in the wild; examples are the many attractive plants with variegated leaves, caused by an inability to produce the full amount of chlorophyll needed for efficient photosynthesis. Fitness for cultivation in the garden or as a house-plant is not always the same as fitness for survival in the wild.

FAULTY TREATMENT

The second factor, faulty treatment, includes too little attention or too much, overfeeding, underfeeding or simply wrong feeding, unhealthy and unsuitable conditions, and stress. If the advice on these subjects given in this book is followed, the risks to health arising from faulty treatment should be, if not eliminated, at least very much reduced. Something else which can give rise to trouble is the failure to take certain precautions to prevent infection occurring. An all too common way for infection to gain entrance is through wounds left by careless pruning, and such wounds should be given proper care (see pages 163–4). Another source of infection comes from attacks by insect and other pests, which by their gnawing may open the way for invasion by disease, or by their piercing and sucking may actually inject harmful germs into the sap-stream. Try to deal with pests as soon as the first signs of attack are seen, so that no serious infestation is allowed to occur (see pages 188–205).

Apart from encouraging healthy and sturdy growth, the biggest contribution you can make to the prevention of illness is to be as careful about hygiene outdoors as indoors. In particular, never leave decaying leaves, prunings or other rubbish lying about to provide a home for pests and disease germs. If it is reasonably soft and not obviously infected, put it on the compost heap; if it is too hard and woody to rot down easily, or clearly diseased, burn it.

DISEASES

Even genetically sound and well-treated plants living in clean and pleasant surroundings are sometimes the victims of disease germs. There are large numbers of these, some of which will attack a wide range of different plants, and others of which confine their unwanted attentions to one kind only. It would be impossible in this book to deal with them all. We will therefore restrict ourselves to those which are particularly responsible for the ailments of infancy.

There are four kinds of pathogen which cause the maladies from which children suffer: fungi, bacteria, viruses and parasitic threadworms. All four of these groups of organisms also attack plants, some more severely than others.

Probably those that cause the most trouble to young plants are those that are the least damaging to young children, that is to say the fungi. The first and potentially the most lethal disease to attack seedlings at their earliest stage is that known as 'damping off', caused by a fungus that invades the vulnerable young stem at soil level and causes it to collapse completely, so that the plant topples over. The spread of the disease can be horrifyingly rapid, every plant in a tray of seedlings being wiped out within an hour or two. Since the fungus flourishes in overcrowded conditions and where the surface of the soil is constantly wet, preventive measures include sowing sparingly, thinning and/or pricking out early, and not watering too much. The use of sterilized seed compost (see page 77) should prevent the disease from occurring, but if it does the spread may be halted by removing the dead seedlings and then watering with Cheshunt compound, zineb or captan.

Bacterial diseases, which can be very serious in humans and other animals (though most bacteria are in fact benign organisms essential to life), are less common in plants. Few are of great concern, at any rate in temperate climates, being confined to such things as bacterial canker of plums and cherries, spotting of leaves, and soft rot of stems and bulbs, reducing them to a slimy mass. Since the bacteria concerned cannot easily break through a plant's protective outer layer, they enter through wounds or pores. Once inside the plant tissues, though, they cannot be reached by spraying. The only thing to do, therefore, is to remove and destroy infected plants, clean any pots or benches they may have been in or on, and use sterilized soil or compost.

Related to the threadworms which can cause so much itching and misery to small children are the eelworms, which are parasites of several different kinds of plants. They are particularly damaging to potatoes and tomatoes, the roots of which can become infested with the tiny, voracious, thread-like creatures, which sap the plant's vitality, causing the growth to become weak and sickly and seriously reducing the crop. Probably the best way for the amateur to counter the menace is to practise a strict rotation, as sensible farmers do, not growing the same crop in the same place for another three or four years. Even that may not be the perfect solution to the problem, however, since cysts, which are the pinhead-sized dead bodies of suicidal female eelworms, each containing hundreds of eggs, may remain capable for many years of disgorging hordes of live and hungry young as soon as a new crop is planted to whet their appetites. Commercial growers of tomatoes and other affected crops have for many years sterilized their soil by means of steam or chemicals to destroy the tiny pests, but many are now turning to soil-less cultivation, feeding the plants with a solution of various salts, because they find it more reliable and cheaper. Meanwhile the plant-breeders are beginning to have some success in developing new varieties with genetically built-in resistance to the worms.

The fourth group of disease-causing organisms is the viruses, so small that they cannot be seen under an ordinary microscope and only able to live by invading the cells of animals or plants and interfering with their functioning. These viruses are responsible for some of the gravest illnesses of childhood, such as polio. Nowadays, at any rate in medically advanced societies, many of these one-time killers and cripplers have been more or less eradicated, thanks to inoculation against them in infancy; the same is true of some of the bacterial diseases as well. Unfortunately, though there have been a few successful experiments with plants (for instance the inoculation of tomatoes against the debilitating mosaic virus), we are still a long way from the day when plants will be given their routine jabs against illnesses as children are now.

Meanwhile virus infections are among the most threatening to the health of our cultivated plants. Some plants show a certain degree of tolerance to viral interference with the normal functioning of their cells, but a great many do not. Any part – leaves, flowers, fruit – or the entire plant may show symptoms of distress: mottling or irregular patterns, striping, discoloration, distortion, stunted growth or even death. Since any affected plant is a possible source of infection to others, and viruses can be spread so easily – by sap-sucking pests, by knives or other tools, by seed or on the hands – and since there are at present no known cures, the best advice that can be given is to remove *and burn* any plant that shows symptoms of virus infection. Be careful to sterilize – over a flame or by dipping in spirit – all pruning knives and secateurs, to prevent infection being spread. As an added precaution, buy only approved or certified disease-free stock from a reputable dealer.

Choice of food

As EXPLAINED in chapter 8, three elements are of particular importance for plant nutrition, and need to be readily available if growth is to be strong and healthy. These three elements are nitrogen, phosphorus and potassium, and each of them can be obtained in several different forms of fertilizer, organic and inorganic. To help you choose the best for your plants, here is a list of the types generally obtainable, together with recommended rates of use and possible advantages and disadvantages.

ORGANIC NITROGEN FERTILIZERS

Hoof and horn meal is made by grinding up the hoofs and horns obtained from slaughteryards. It comes in different grades, according to the fineness or coarseness of the grinding. The finer the mixture is ground, the larger the amount of nitrogen readily available. Since hoof is a richer source of nitrogen than horn, the proportion of hoof to horn in the mixture also makes a difference to the amount of nitrogen available. A good mixture contains about 14 per cent nitrogen; the grade used for most purposes, particularly for potting composts, is called ⅛ inch (3mm) grist. Like all other organic fertilizers, hoof and horn meal has to be broken down by bacteria into simpler substances before it can give the soluble nitrogen salts which plant roots are able to assimilate. That is why it is so often said to be slow-acting, and therefore – because the nitrogen in it is not so easily available and as a consequence not so easily wasted – more economical than the inorganic nitrogenous fertilizers, in spite of its higher cost. It is true that the larger particles can take quite a long time to be broken down, but the finer particles can yield a good quantity of available nitrogen salts quite rapidly if the soil is in the right condition and contains plenty of beneficial bacteria. So the truth is that hoof and horn fertilizer, or at least a large proportion of it, is a great deal quicker-acting than many people think. It is excellent for potting composts.

Dried blood, sold in the form of a rather coarse powder, is a quick-acting organic food, varying somewhat in its formula, like other organic substances, but usually containing between 12 and 15 per cent nitrogen. It also contains phosphate (about 2.5% P_2O_5) and compounds of potassium, calcium, sodium and other elements, notably iron, which is a vital ingredient of haemoglobin, the red pigment in blood. Like hoof and horn meal, it is a by-product of slaughteryards. In spite of the fact that it is one of the most expensive fertilizers you can buy, it still has a steady sale among old-fashioned gardeners, many of whom swear by it and credit it with almost magical powers. When blood could be obtained for next to nothing (or even for nothing) from a local slaughteryard it could, properly treated, provide a cheap source of nitrogen for use during the growing season. Now, processed and packaged, it is expensive.

Fish meal is another organic source of nitrogen (around 10% N), together with phosphate (variable, but often about 3% P_2O_5) and some potash (2% K_2O or less). When fish was more plentiful and the trimmings from it readily available, it made a cheap fertilizer after the oil had been extracted and what remained had been dried and ground down to an easily handled form. Now, with fish getting scarcer and the waste being bought up by the manufacturers of pet food, fish meal, like dried blood, is becoming expensive. It also varies greatly in the amount of plant foods it contains. The only thing that can be guaranteed about it is the smell.

If you do use fish meal, apply it to the soil in winter or early spring, so that it has time to mellow before sowing time; in its fresh state it can seriously interfere with germination and damage young roots. One other point needs watching: as soon as you have applied fish meal to the ground (at between 2 and 4oz to the square yard (60–125g to the square metre)), fork it well into the soil. It may not seem very appetizing to us, but birds find it irresistible and will greedily devour every scrap if you leave it spread over the surface for them to get at.

Poultry manure has the reputation of being 'strong'. Sometimes it is; indeed, used fresh it can scorch tender young roots and inhibit germination, because of its high proportion of instantly available nitrogen. On the other hand, some samples are anything but strong – except perhaps in their smell – and contribute very little to the soil other than a tendency to make it sticky and sour. The nutrient contents vary so widely according to the way the poultry have been fed, the conditions in which they have been kept, the nature of the litter with which their droppings are mixed (peat, straw, sawdust, wood shavings or what-have-you), and whether the manure has been protected from the weather or not, that without a full analysis it is impossible to tell what its value is. If you have a free supply, because you keep poultry, or have a neighbour who does, or live near a poultry farm, it would of course be silly not to make use of the manure; there are not many things to be had for nothing these days. Some people dry the droppings, pulverize them, mix them with bonfire ash and soil and/or sand, and apply the result as a top-dressing to strongly growing vegetables such as cabbages and onions, at the rate of ¼–½lb per square yard (125–250g per square metre). Because of the variability of poultry manure, though, and its possible dangers in concentrated form (particularly if it comes from a deep-litter house, where the hens may have been fed or injected with antibiotics), it is usually best mixed with other material on the compost heap, where it can be valuable as an activator, to speed up the rotting down process.

Farmyard manure is even more variable. If you can get it locally at a not too extortionate price, it can be excellent as a soil-conditioner, applied either direct or after being composted with other material (see page 29). It is, however, quite unreliable for specific use as a fertilizer, since its nitrogen content – and for that matter its content of the other two main elements – tends to vary from rather low to practically non-existent.

Other things available as waste products, and therefore cheap, are sometimes used as organic sources of nitrogen, but the main ones are as listed above, of which by far the most important is hoof and horn meal. Champions of organic gardening may, however, have a problem – spiritual rather than scientific – in using such materials, as explained under the heading 'Do vegetarian diets suit young plants?' (page 143).

INORGANIC NITROGEN FERTILIZERS

Sulphate of ammonia (otherwise called ammonium sulphate) is the commonest and cheapest inorganic nitrogenous fertilizer. It used to be merely a by-product of gas works and some manufacturing processes, but now it is made synthetically in large quantities. Unlike the widely variable organic fertilizers, sulphate of ammonia is a very predictable and uniform product, of which just over one-fifth is nitrogen (21% N). So long as the soil has a good clay content the nitrogen, in its ammonium form, is not easily washed away, because it is held by the clay particles. In poorer, sandy soils, though, it can disappear quite quickly, since there is nothing much to hang on to it. It is fairly rapid in its action, though not so rapid as fertilizers containing the nitrate form of nitrogen, and so is useful to give a boost to leafy vegetables such as cabbages during the growing season when the soil is warm enough for bacteria to get to work turning the ammonia into nitrate so that plants can use it. When the soil is too cold to liven up the bacteria, the ammonium form changes very slowly, so very little is lost.

There are two possible disadvantages in using sulphate of ammonia. It can scorch leaves if dropped on them, and roots too if it comes in contact with them in a concentrated state. It should therefore be used on damp soil so it will soon be dissolved; if the soil is dry it should be well watered in. The other disadvantage is that it can, if used too often, make certain soils very acid, because the ammonium nitrogen dislodges calcium from clay, so that it forms soluble calcium sulphate; and since calcium keeps soil sweet, its loss turns the soil sour. So it is unwise to use sulphate of ammonia where the ground tends to be acid, especially in the vegetable garden if members of the cabbage family suffer from club-root disease, which flourishes in calcium-deficient soils. Where there is no such problem, a normal rate of use during spring and summer is ½–1oz a square yard (15–30g a square metre). A useful liquid feed can be made up by dissolving a teaspoonful in a gallon (4.5 litres) of water.

Sulphate of ammonia has the advantage that, unlike many other nitrogenous fertilizers, it can be easily stored without deterioration.

Nitrate of soda is quicker in its action than sulphate of ammonia, because all the nitrogen in it is in the nitrate form and so is instantly available to plant roots as soon as it is dissolved in the soil moisture. Just under one-sixth of it is nitrogen (15.5% N). Because it gets to work so quickly, it is very useful to give a boost to plants, particularly green vegetables, that are hanging fire after a spell of cold weather. If applied between rows of plants at the rate of ½oz to the square yard (15g a square metre), it can produce spectacular results in a very short time. Because this fertilizer contains sodium as well as nitrogen, it is excellent for crops like beetroot and celery, which enjoy sodium in their diet.

Nitrate of soda has a few possible disadvantages. Because nitrate is so soluble it can very quickly be washed out of the soil by rain; so do not use it except during the growing season when the plants can take it in, or you will be pouring goodness, and money, down the drain.

Be careful not to overdo the dose. If given in too large a quantity, or too often, nitrate of soda can damage the texture of some soils by breaking down the crumb structure, so destroying the vital air spaces and preventing roots from breathing properly.

Storage can be an awkward problem. Nitrate fertilizers take up a great deal of moisture from the air, and soon degenerate into a soggy mass unless they are kept in sealed, airtight containers.

Ammonium nitrate is a single fertilizer, of which just over one-third is nitrogen (34.5% N). It is a highly concentrated source of nitrogen, half in the ammonium form and half as nitrate. Since it contains nothing but plant food, it is an excellent way of feeding nitrogen, not only in instantly available form but in somewhat longer-lasting form as well. It is used considerably by commercial growers, but is not readily obtainable by amateur gardeners, since it is somewhat tricky stuff to handle and rather expensive – though because of its concentration it can be used more sparingly than the other nitrogenous fertilizers so far mentioned: at the rate of about 1oz to 3 or 4 square yards (30g to 3 or 4 square metres). It soon becomes semi-liquid unless it is kept in a tightly sealed plastic bag or other airtight container. Like sulphate of ammonia, it has a tendency to acidify the soil.

'Nitro-chalk' is manufactured by mixing ammonium nitrate with chalk so as to prevent it from turning the soil acid. It contains just over one-fifth nitrogen (21% N), and because of its combination of ammonia and nitrate it gives both immediate and more long-term results. It can be used in spring and summer as a top-dressing, particularly in the vegetable garden, at the rate of ¼–½oz to the square yard (7–15g a square metre). Being granular, it is much easier to spread than ammonium nitrate. It must be kept in an airtight container.

Chilean potash nitrate is actually a mixed nitrate of sodium and potassium; indeed, it is sometimes called Chilean nitrate of soda. As a 'compound fertilizer' it contains about one-seventh nitrogen (15% N) and one-tenth potash (10% K_2O). It can be used – particularly in the spring, when nitrogen alone might produce soft growth, easily damaged by late frosts – either as a top-dressing at the rate of 10z to the square yard (30g a square metre) or as a liquid feed made by mixing 1 teaspoonful to a gallon (4.5 litres) of water. It too takes moisture from the air and so should be kept sealed in an airtight container when not in use.

Nitrate of potash is a much purer, but considerably more expensive fertilizer, containing both nitrogen (12–14% N) and potash (44–46% K_2O). Dissolved in water at the rate of ½oz to the gallon (15g to 4.5 litres), it is useful as a liquid feed for greenhouse plants. It too must be kept in an airtight container.

A few other nitrogenous fertilizers such as urea, found originally in urine but now produced synthetically, are sometimes used by specialists, but the ones listed above are those most available to, and suitable for, amateurs.

ORGANIC PHOSPHATE FERTILIZERS

Bone meal is a popular, readily available and fairly cheap organic source of phosphate. It is made by removing the fat, but not the gelatin, from bones and then grinding them down until they are reduced to a fine meal. Like so many organic fertilizers, it varies quite a lot in composition, according to the source of the bones and the method of processing them, but can contain over one-fifth phosphate (20–25% P_2O_5) in addition to some useful nitrogen in quick-acting form (4% N), which comes from the gelatin. It can be used at the rate of 40z to the square yard (125g a square metre) at any time from late autumn to early spring; the phosphate, being in insoluble form, is released slowly and steadily through the action of soil organisms. Many people sprinkle a handful or two into planting holes to help the growth of new roots. Bone meal may also be used, at 40z (113g) a bushel (8 gallons/36 litres), in potting composts, if you prefer organic material to the more usual (and more effective) superphosphate; the trouble is that bone meal does not get along at all well with the lime in the compost, whereas superphosphate and lime work together splendidly.

There is a very real danger in using bone meal. It can carry salmonella, which causes food poisoning, or even typhoid, and in rare cases the horrible disease anthrax. To be safe, do not buy bone meal unless it has been sterilized, or steamed; as an added precaution wear gloves when handling it.

Steamed bone flour is not so commonly used as bone meal, from which it differs in having had all the gelatin removed as well as the fat. That means that very little nitrogen is left (1% N or less) but that the phosphate content is increased (25-30% P_2O_5). As with bone meal, the phosphate is in an insoluble form, but because bone flour is, as its name implies, much more finely ground, the soil organisms can get to work on it quicker, so it is somewhat faster in action. It can be applied to the soil at between 2 and 4oz a square yard (60–125g a square metre) in winter or early spring.

Because of the steaming process through which it has gone, bone flour should be free from disease germs. It is less readily available, and more expensive, than bone meal, but it is pleasanter to handle and less smelly. Knowledgeable people who mix up their own fertilizers have found that the inclusion of some bone flour stops the mixture from caking together and keeps it dry and free-flowing.

Fish meal, already dealt with under nitrogenous fertilizers, also contains a small amount of phosphate (around 3% P_2O_5). For rate of use, and precautions to be taken, see page 212.

INORGANIC PHOSPHATE FERTILIZERS

Superphosphate (otherwise known as superphosphate of lime) has been shown over many years, in large numbers of tests, to be as near the ideal phosphate fertilizer as one can get. It is completely reliable, contains just about one-fifth phosphate (18–20% P_2O_5), and is a standard ingredient in seed and potting composts. The more extreme champions of organic methods of growing say some very nasty things about superphosphate, because it is manufactured by grinding rock phosphate and then treating it with sulphuric acid, and hence is 'artificial'.

Because of the treatment it has received, superphosphate is a quick-acting fertilizer, with a high proportion of soluble phosphate, so it is particularly suitable to stimulate root growth in seed-beds, where it will give newly emerging seedlings just the right start in life if applied at the rate of 2oz a square yard (60g a square metre) and lightly raked in just before sowing. It is excellent in the vegetable garden, where it helps to produce magnificent carrots and other root crops. For its use in seed and potting composts, see page 78.

In case you should think that because of the process it has gone through to make it quick-acting the phosphate not immediately taken up by the plant will rapidly wash away, it should be pointed out that when it touches the soil it is soon converted into a less soluble form. This in turn is slowly released into the water in the soil, and so can be used by plants in small instalments over a period of time. It therefore combines the properties of a quick-acting and a slow-acting fertilizer.

Triple superphosphate is a more concentrated form, used largely by commercial growers. It does not, as its name might suggest, contain three times as much phosphate as the ordinary superphosphate, but only just over twice as much (about 44% P_2O_5). It is not normally available for amateurs, and its extra expense is not justified for their purposes.

Basic slag used to be a very cheap source of phosphates, since it is a waste product from steel works. Now it is not so cheap, partly because of the decline in steel manufacture and partly because it is sold to fertilizer companies, who put it through grinding processes, package it, and market it under a brand name through garden suppliers. Its value depends to a considerable extent on how finely it is ground, and its composition varies a good deal. It may contain anything from a tenth to a sixth phosphate (10–18% P_2O_5) in an insoluble form, which is only very slowly turned into a food that roots can absorb. Since it has no immediate effect, it should be applied during the autumn or early in the winter, at a rate of 4–8oz a square yard (125–250g a square metre); then a proportion of it will be starting to be usable by plants when the growing season comes around.

Because of its considerable calcium content, basic slag is a useful phosphate fertilizer for acid soils. To avoid an adverse chemical reaction, never apply it to the ground at the same time as lime.

ORGANIC POTASH FERTILIZERS

Wood ash may, when fresh, contain anything between one-twentieth and nearly one-sixth potash (5–15% K_2O). Unfortunately the potash is in such readily soluble form that a few heavy rains can wash practically all of it away. So keep the ashes from bonfires under cover till they are needed; otherwise you may be wasting your time applying to the soil something that is pretty well useless. If you find it difficult to cover the ashes, shovel them into a dustbin with a well-fitting lid; if it is a plastic dustbin, be careful to let the ashes cool down first, because if they are put in hot they can easily ruin the plastic.

On light, sandy soils, where potassium deficiency is most likely to occur, ashes may be sprinkled on the ground at the rate of 4oz or so to the square yard (125g to the square metre); do this in the autumn or winter, so that the possibly caustic nature of the fresh ashes will have had time to disappear by the time next year's growing season begins. Before applying the ashes to the soil, many people first mix them with sifted earth, which makes them easier to handle.

Do not use wood ash as a dressing on heavy soil; it might cake the clay particles together so that the surface becomes sticky and difficult to rake into a suitable condition for sowing seeds, or form a crust which does not allow air to penetrate into the soil so that roots can breathe. And because of the other components of wood ash besides potash, it is unwise to give heavy dressings to chalky soils; such dressings may make the ground even more alkaline. The best thing to do with ashes if you have heavy or chalky soil is to use them on the compost heap (see page 29), where they will enrich the mixture, lose their caustic properties, and retain the bulk of their potash through absorption by the other ingredients of the heap, so that instead of being washed away the potash is to a large extent held in readiness for when it is needed by plants.

There are few other organic sources of potash, though it is present in small amounts in fertilizers which mainly supply other foods, such as dried blood, and in processed seaweed, sold as a dry powder.

INORGANIC POTASH FERTILIZERS

Sulphate of potash is an excellent and completely reliable inorganic source of potassium in an easily available form that can be used at once by plants. About half of it is pure potash (48–50% K_2O). However, though this is readily soluble its composition is such that it is not easily washed from the soil. It is manufactured by grinding and processing natural rock deposits rich in potash. Until a few years ago, it seemed as if there were enough of these rock deposits in many parts of the world for the supply to last indefinitely. Now it is predicted that before long supplies will start to run low, and prices will rise steeply. For the present, sulphate of potash is one of the most widely used fertilizers by professional and amateur growers. It may be applied to the soil at the rate of ½–1oz a square yard (15–30g a square metre) at any time before sowing or planting, and is generally used in combination with other fertilizers. For quick results, it may be dissolved in water (1oz (30g) to the gallon (4.5 litres)) and used as a liquid feed in cases of potash deficiency; if the soil is not already damp, water it thoroughly beforehand, to avoid damaging tender roots.

Sulphate of potash is a standard ingredient in the most widely used and successful seed and potting composts (see page 78).

Muriate of potash (otherwise known as potassium chloride) is used a great deal by commercial vegetable-growers, but not so much by amateur gardeners. It is a highly concentrated fertilizer, containing up to three-fifths potash (60% K_2O), and is cheaper than the sulphate; but it is not so easy to store, is less convenient to handle, and can do considerable damage to young plants, particularly at the seedling stage. To reduce the risk, apply it only to damp soil. Use no more than ½oz square yard (15g a square metre).

Chilean potash nitrate, already dealt with under nitrogenous fertilizers (see page 216), contains somewhat varying amounts of potash (around 10% K_2O) and may be used, as described, at the rate of 1oz to the square yard (15g a square metre) in the spring. Do not use it in the autumn, because the nitrate will be washed away during the winter; worse, it might stimulate too much growth, which frosts can damage.

Nitrate of potash, also dealt with under nitrogenous fertilizers, contains considerably more potash (44–46% K_2O). See page 216 for instructions on the method of using and storing it.

INDEX